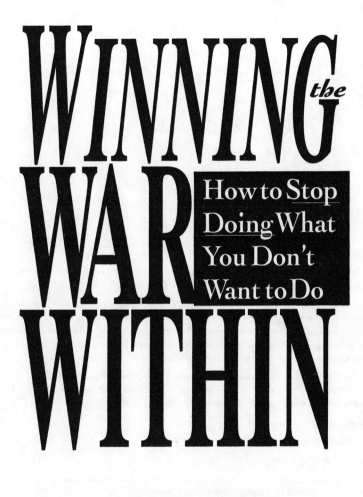

WINNING the WAR WITHIN

How to Stop Doing What You Don't Want to Do

Peter Wilkes

INTERVARSITY PRESS
DOWNERS GROVE, ILLINOIS 60515

InterVarsity Press® is the book-publishing division of InterVarsity Christian Fellowship®, a student movement active on campus at hundreds of universities, colleges and schools of nursing in the United States of America, and a member movement of the International Fellowship of Evangelical Students. For information about local and regional activities, write Public Relations Dept., InterVarsity Christian Fellowship, 6400 Schroeder Rd., P.O. Box 7895, Madison, WI 53707-7895.

All Scripture quotations, unless otherwise indicated, are taken from the HOLY BIBLE, NEW INTERNATIONAL VERSION®. NIV®. Copyright © 1973, 1978, 1984 by International Bible Society. Used by permission of Zondervan Publishing House. All rights reserved.

Cover illustration: Roberta Polfus

ISBN 0-8308-1605-4

Printed in the United States of America ∞

Library of Congress Cataloging-in-Publication Data

Wilkes, Peter.
      Winning the war within: how to stop doing what you don't want to
   do/Peter Wilkes.
         p.   cm.
      Includes bibliographical references.
      ISBN 0-8308-1605-4 (alk. paper)
      1. Compulsive behavior—Religious aspects—Christianity.
   I. Title.
   BV4598.7.W55   1995
   248.4—dc20   94-45404
                                                          CIP

17	16	15	14	13	12	11	10	9	8	7	6	5	4	3	2	1
09	08	07	06	05	04	03	02	01	00	99	98	97	96	95		

To my children
Simon, Jonathan and Elisabeth,
who taught me how to be a dad

Preface

Nowadays just about everyone in our society speaks the language of psychology. This poses a considerable challenge for Christians, who have to test secular trends by the straight edge of the Bible.

Our response has not been uniform. Some Christians have accepted the ideas of psychology uncritically, undermining the faith that supports them. Others have attacked the whole discipline, dismissing important truths that have been uncovered by the practice of psychotherapy.

As a pastor with a heavy counseling load, I have looked for guidance on how to approach psychological models and techniques from a Christian perspective. For the most part I have looked in vain. Some of the best Christian authors I have read seem too intimidated by psychology to question its claims and assumptions adequately; others lack a sufficient grasp of theology to offer a helpful biblical critique. Few seem ready to think deeply and radically about the relationship between psychology and Christianity.

My contacts with psychotherapists have been stimulating; at

times I have found myself working with them at the cutting edge of where they too were learning. Because our emotional and spiritual well-being are intertwined, I have found my pastoral experiences highly relevant to what I believe is psychotherapy's goal—the cure of souls.

These counseling experiences have given me the confidence to write this book, which includes some radical ideas for an outsider to the field of psychology. The personality-role theory I develop, for example, owes as much to biblical theology as to psychology.

Because I am deeply convinced of the authority of the Bible, readers will find that my ideas are continually tested against Scripture. This does not mean, however, that I stick only to conventional biblical interpretations; some theologians will, no doubt, end up as angry at me as some psychologists.

My answer to both groups is that I have worked out my ideas with real people, many of whom have found wholeness with God's help. What I have learned I pass on in the hope that it will stimulate others to grow also.

I believe in the healing power of the Christian life. I believe in the value of prayer, fellowship, servanthood and the development of Christian character. All of these things are found first and foremost in healthy churches; indeed, I have learned most by sharing the leadership of a congregation committed to growth under the Word. The church is the primary place we find healing. Throughout this book I make no bones about the necessity to be active in the body of Christ.

I have many people to thank. They include the persons whose stories you will find here. Although I have changed details to protect their anonymity, their lives are recorded here for all to learn from. I also thank the elders and my fellow pastors of South Hills Community Church for their support, stimulation and love. Not least I owe thanks to my secretary Judy Keister, and to my wife for her endless patience.

1
DOING WHAT WE DON'T WANT TO DO

. . . .

Ted and May *were very much in love when they* got married. They seemed to fit each other like tailor-made clothes. As the years passed, however, they became concerned about problems between them. That's when they came to see me.

The first issue they discussed with me was the rearing of their three children. May put significant pressure on them to excel in academics, sports and every other area of life. Ted, on the other hand, spoiled the children. He wanted their approval and won it by undermining May's orders in subtle ways.

The second problem they identified was money. Ted was a skilled computer programmer and made a good salary. Yet in spite of their ample income, they were always in debt. May tried to run the finances, but Ted undermined every plan she made for their financial security. He would invest and spend money freely, never seeming to know where it had gone.

A surprising third issue arose as we talked—a perplexing role reversal between the typically strong-willed May and the usually passively resistant Ted that occurred when they took up ballroom dancing. Ted, who had turned out to be a very good dancer, acted like a different person on the dance floor. He became masterful and dominant, imperious in his leading of steps. May didn't have much rhythm, but she enjoyed melting into Ted's arms and being carried away. The problem was that after an evening of dancing was over, Ted would sometimes shout at May angrily over an insignificant comment. By the time they came to me, these angry scenes, though still infrequent, were becoming violent. They spoke about this problem as "Ted's temper."

Ted and May were concerned that they couldn't seem to change their patterns of behavior. May didn't want to be so domineering with Ted and the kids, and Ted didn't want to undermine May's work with the children or their finances. Ted felt especially ashamed of his inability to control his behavior. But both seemed stuck in destructive ways of acting.

Ted and May will return later in the book as I explore how they came to develop habits that they couldn't break. Unfortunately, their experience is only too well known to many of us. What we don't want to do, we do anyway. What we do want to do, we just can't seem to make a regular part of our lives.

Take Derek, a young businessman I know. In his personal life he is a gentle soul, sensitive and rather passive. But buried inside is a tiger that has driven him into an intensely high-pressure career as a stockbroker of the gambling sort. Once after confiding to a friend how stressful his work was, he paused and added, "But I couldn't live without it." He says he feels compelled to keep high on adrenaline to satisfy some atavistic craving inside.

Then there's Sally, the saddest person I ever met. Sally was a young mother of four whose husband, Clark, met her when he found her sleeping in the trash behind a bar. He took Sally under his wing and weaned her from an addiction to crack cocaine. In time she opened her heart to faith in Christ; they fell in love, married and started a family.

As time went by the excitement of Sally's new life died down and was replaced by mundane routine. For a while she felt bored. Then her four children were born, and Sally's boredom was replaced by stress. Under the pressures of raising a family, she started to cope by resorting to former patterns of behavior, slipping away now and then to get high with old friends. One day she decided to leave her family altogether. Clark searched for her for days, found her and persuaded her to return. This happened several times. On each occasion she seemed eager to return, but in time she always ended up back in the drug community.

When Clark and Sally began meeting with me, it became clear that she really did want to change and have a normal family life. Many times she had tried, really tried, to be a good wife and mother; but she was wrestling with something inside that always overcame her and dragged her down.

Clark wanted Sally to come home again but was afraid of exposing their children to another experience of abandonment. We decided to proceed slowly, working with Sally to build a new lifestyle before allowing her to return to her family. She moved into the home of a Christian couple and, over the months, seemed to be recovering.

One day Sally's hosts went on vacation, leaving her alone in the house. Soon afterward their neighbors called the church because they had become alarmed at the noisy parties Sally was throwing. Her old "friends" had made contact once again.

The next time Sally came to see me, she was gripped by despair. "I've just got to go back," she said plaintively through the dark cloud of hair over her face. "I can't help it." Although Sally loved her children and yearned to return, she was locked in a desperate inner battle with herself that she was losing.

We talked for a long time, but I was unable to reach her. The last I heard she was living on the streets, making money from men who picked her up and spending everything she earned on drugs. I wonder how long she'll survive.

Inner Compulsion

Sally was a slave to drugs. Since most of us are not drug addicts, it would be easy to think that her experience is irrelevant to ours. Much more often than we think, however, our actions are just as compulsive as those of any drug addict. Many of us, for example, struggle with lust. Advertising executives know this and use it to manipulate us into buying all kinds of products, from clothes to cars. Most of us don't want to be influenced by lust; in fact, we often fight it. Nevertheless, the power of lust is great, and under its compulsion we do things that we regret later.

As we look back, we feel we were somehow overcome by a force inside ourselves that we were powerless to resist. We may go on repeating this experience many times, knowing all the while how foolish it is. The inner compulsion that drives a drug addict on—the sense of being overcome by something inside— is driving our behavior too.

The apostle Paul was no stranger to the inner struggle. Looking back on his life, he reflects that "at one time we too were . . . enslaved by all kinds of passions and pleasures" (Titus 3:3). Indeed, all of us have experienced the pain of Paul's cry: "I have the desire to do what is good, but I cannot carry it out. . . . What a wretched man I am! Who will rescue me from this body of death?" (Romans 7:18-24).

Christians often feel uncomfortable admitting to compulsive behavior because we mistakenly believe that our faith should eliminate such problems. We love to hear testimonies of people who have been set free from evil habits by the power of God. Such miracles of grace do occur, and we should rejoice over them. The danger lies in making the miracle our standard—in expecting ourselves to be set free from all compulsions and to live in permanent victory.

Preachers and other Christian leaders who repeatedly exhort us to stop sinning may inadvertently reinforce our unrealistic expectations. Ashamed of our struggles, we pretend that they have disappeared, but secretly we feel worse than ever. In private we keep trying to master our problems on our own with self-discipline, only to keep failing. Ultimately we reach a quiet despair.

It would be wonderful if, after receiving God's forgiveness, Christians were immediately freed from destructive habits. But the reality is that alcoholism, child abuse, gossip and other compulsive behaviors are found inside the church; judging by the New Testament, it has probably always been so. We read of drunkenness at the Lord's Supper (1 Corinthians 11:21), of sexual immorality (1 Corinthians 6:13-14), of "passionate lust" (1 Thessalonians 4:5), to mention just three examples. The early church was not a compulsion-free community. Many believers had a hard time throwing off old habits.

We, too, eagerly learn the Bible's teachings, only to discover how hard they are to apply. Paul's desperate entreaty in Romans 7 is often interpreted by Bible commentators as the cry of the Christian soul. This alone suggests that Christians can behave as compulsively as anyone else.

I have listened with pity to Christian men and women—many of them in full-time ministry—confessing to lifelong struggles with compulsive behavior: a young preacher, effective and gifted in the pulpit, who had been wrestling with anger so severe that he ended up beating his wife, scarring her face; an older friend who had been hiding a secret drinking problem; a father who had been committing incest with his daughter for ten years. These things go on in churches. Pretending they don't only compounds the problem.

These situations underline the terrible power of inner compulsions. None of these people wanted to be what they were. Often they were serious, well-taught Christians, bitterly ashamed of their actions. They longed for deliverance. Some had contemplated suicide. Others had tried miracle cures. Still others had tried to overcome their problems by attempting to exorcise demons. Usually these approaches did not work; even when they did, the release they offered was often only temporary.

Because only extreme kinds of compulsive behavior usually get discussed, we can get the impression that only tormented people are driven by inner compulsions. The truth is that most of us struggle with compulsive behavior.

We may become compulsive about—that is, addicted to—all kinds of things. Here are just a few of the most common:

☐ stress
☐ control
☐ submission
☐ anger
☐ overeating
☐ alcohol
☐ drugs
☐ work
☐ money
☐ pornography
☐ sex
☐ fear
☐ self-pity
☐ perfection
☐ selfishness
☐ emotions
☐ approval by others
☐ rules

Behind them all lies a common experience that my helpless, drug-addict friend described poignantly to me: "Do you think I want to do this? I know it's stupid. I love my kids and wish I could go home, but it's no use. I try to change, but I can't. I hate this part of me that wants to go away and do drugs. I am my own worst enemy. I wish I could die."

Compulsive behavior simply means being overcome by something inside—a feeling of helplessness in the face of something that seems irresistible. Which of us has not been appalled at our own weakness as we succumb to the same temptation time and time again? How often have each of us settled for a discreet acceptance of a bad habit and despaired of ever winning a victory? Isn't this the real reason our experience of Christianity is so mediocre? Isn't this what makes us cynical about God himself and Christianity in general? We urgently need a better understanding of compulsive behavior in Christian terms—an understanding that's consistent with the Bible.

Looking for Help
Why do we do the things that we do? That's the very question that psychology attempts to answer. So it would seem that we should be able to turn to psychology as a source of help for understanding and eliminating compulsive behavior.

Indeed, psychology offers many answers about why we do the things we do. The problem is that there are too many answers—often contradictory ones. Following Freud, psychoanalysts speak of unconscious drives deep in our primal being, fed by sexual desires toward our parents. Behavioral psychologists insist that *all* our actions are compulsive, for we are nothing more than biological machines. Jungians argue that we are influenced by a collective unconscious. Alcoholics Anonymous insists that compulsive behavior comes from denial of alcoholism.

Sometimes there seem to be as many answers as there are psychologists. Yet not everyone who seeks help in counseling finds it. Why? For believers other troubling questions arise: Do all of these psychological models affirm a biblical understanding of human nature? If not, how can a Christian wholeheartedly engage in the counseling process?

I believe that a new approach to overcoming compulsive behavior is needed—an approach that both makes use of current psychological theories *and* affirms a biblical understanding of human nature. Such an approach is the subject of the rest of this book.

2
WHICH I
IS ME?

• • • • • • •

Shakespeare only *told part of the truth when* he wrote that all the world's a stage. The world inside each of our heads is one too. There I am the only actor. I try on many faces and play many roles. I find many of these roles come easily; some I was taught as a child, while others were learned as an adult. On the other hand, I find some roles difficult or even painful to perform; I play them to please or appease others in my life. Some of these are roles that I hate but cannot seem to resist under certain circumstances.

Social roles are no minor part of our emotional makeup. The way we speak, think and act is largely determined by our environment. The ultimate example is the "wild child" that appears occasionally. Lost as infants, these children were adopted and raised by animals. Such children are more animal than human. They speak in animal sounds and behave as animals.

To be sure, we begin life hard-wired in certain ways, like an intricate machine with powerful processing capabilities but no data to process. As life unfolds, it brings data to us in the form of experiences, a process that starts even in the womb. As we absorb experiences, they are transformed from raw memories into processed memories[1] organized by the brain into related groups. These processed memories shape our learned responses, which in turn affect what we make of new experiences.

In this way our understanding of ourselves and the world around us evolves. Together, physical hard-wiring, processed memory structure and learned responses form each person's unique personality.

Watching young babies and their mothers interact helps us understand this process. A baby is a learning machine. Picking up cues in her mother's behavior, she quickly learns how to please her and gain the rewards of her approval. She also learns what brings her mother displeasure.

In the earliest stages of childhood, when a child can distinguish "mother" from self, it immediately finds itself confronted with this powerful other with a will the child cannot control. The mother has many expectations of the child, and the great powers she holds of reward and punishment are focused on helping the child to grow and learn. Fueled by the mother's interest and enthusiasm in the discoveries of this emerging self, the child simultaneously practices the motor skills needed to make these discoveries as well as the psychological skills that will later become the capacities of the real self—self-activation, self-expression and creativity. At this stage the quality of mothering is crucial. The mother's ability to pick up the cues and signals from her child's emerging self, her own ease of self-expression and creativity, her imagination—these compose the fertile soil in which the child's real self grows and develops.[2]

Soon the child becomes aware of her father, and once again a new pattern of interaction begins. The baby soon learns what brings rewards from this figure and develops a role as "Daddy's child" to add to its first role of "Mommy's baby."

As the child grows up, she plunges into relationship after relationship, each with different expectations, cues and reward systems. She becomes skilled in learning what roles to play in many different situations. As an adult, some roles stay with her, changing as she develops; others disappear as she no longer uses them. Thus she may eventually try to control her angry, out-of-control self by eliminating it from her list of roles. On the other hand, she may try to bring her sympathetic or analytical self to the fore more often.

This picture of self-role development is not my invention, of course. Psychologist J. F. Masterson summarizes his conclusions on the subject this way: "The real self consists of all our self images plus the ability to relate them to each other and recognize them as forming a single, unique individual. These self images are the images we have of our selves at particular times and in specific situations."[3]

Personality, then, breaks down into a repertoire of roles. How these roles—or "subpersonalities"—take shape depends on each person's unique pattern of memories, learned responses and physical makeup. New roles are continually called forth as others draw new responses from us. It's also true that we move easily between numerous existing roles in our everyday interactions with others.

Sometimes the switch between roles can be dramatic. Once when I was excitedly watching the Forty-Niners win a Superbowl, I got a call from a distressed parishioner. As I listened to her anxious voice, my demeanor quickly changed from wildly cheering football fan to soothing, empathic pastor. At the time I wasn't conscious of making the change. Somehow a central, unifying will passed the baton from Peter the fan to Peter the pastor. I was not two people, but two cooperating parts within a whole.

Every day we slip in and out of roles this way, barely aware of a change because we are so good at doing it. It is the stuff of life.

It is also the stuff of literature. In his perceptive book *Who Am I This Time?* psychologist Jay Martin argues that literature's appeal lies in its portrayal of others' role-playing—the great skill of life. Take one of the most famous literary characters of all time, Cervantes's Don Quixote:

A Manchegan gentleman whose reading
Had turned his head with tales of bleeding
Knights-errant, damsels, love's surprises,
And all the Chivalry's disguises.

"His fantasy was filled with the things that he read," Cervantes writes, "and these did so fully possess his imagination that all that he read [seemed] true, as he counted no history in the world to be so certain." Eventually "he fell into one of the strangest conceits that ever madman stumbled on . . . that he himself should become a knight-errant, and practice all that he had read." He made up his mind that henceforth his name was Don Quixote.[4]

Martin suggests that readers are drawn to Cervantes's character because he does more consciously and flamboyantly what we all do daily—take on different roles.[5] Martin goes on to list other memorable literary characters who do the same: in *Wuthering Heights* Cathy says, "I am Heathcliff"; *Madame Bovary*'s heroine identifies with a whole series of other romantic heroines; in *Crime and Punishment* Raskolnikov decides to act as if he were a Napoleon-like superman; and in *The Adventures of Huckleberry Finn* Huck imitates Tom Sawyer while Tom imitates the heroes of romantic adventure novels.

Not only the characters in fiction reveal our fascination with role-playing; so do some of the novelists themselves. One of today's most respected mystery novelists is Ruth Rendell, who writes under the pen name Barbara Vine. Why two pen names?

The answer is as deep and twisty as a Rendell-Vine plot. She has explained that Ruth was her father's choice of name for her, and Barbara was her mother's. She has been known by both names all her life. And each name embodies a part of her personality.

"Ruth is tougher, colder, more analytical, possibly more aggressive," she has written. "Barbara is more feminine. It is Barbara who sews.

"For a long time I have wanted Barbara to have a voice, as well as Ruth. It would be a softer voice speaking at a slower pace, more sensitive perhaps and more intuitive."[6]

Note that Rendell goes back to her relationships with her parents to explain the source of her roles. As we have seen, that is where role development begins.

Back to Freud

None of these ideas about roles is new to psychology. Psychology as we know it, in fact, began when Freud reframed personality in terms of roles or functions inside the self—ego, id and superego. The fact that Freud was thinking in terms of different selves within the total self is clear from his original German wording. *Ego* is the English translation of *ich,* which simply means "I"; thus there are distinct I's within the self.

The first to take Freud's personality theory further was his associate Paul Federn. He proposed the existence of other personality segments called "ego states" (see appendix 2).[7] Since then a number of psychologists have identified different sets of inner selves to help account for the disruptive tensions we all feel within us. John Bradshaw and others, for example, speak of an "inner child" and an "inner parent."[8]

Because most of us share certain basic physical drives and life experiences, it makes sense that we also share certain types of inner selves—an inner child, an inner parent, a conscience, an emotional self and a sexual self, to name a few. While such categories can help us understand ourselves, however, they can limit us if we stick to them too rigidly. Each person should feel free to identify inner selves that reflect his or her unique pattern of life experiences. In a sense we are like kaleidoscopes made by one hand but turned by many; even though we all contain the same pieces inside, our patterns of interactions with others arrange us each into a different design.[9]

What I have been calling "inner selves" or "roles" actually go by many names among psychologists. As mentioned above, Masterson has called them "self images" and Federn "ego states." Other commonly used names include "inner objects" and "intrapsychic images." None of these terms is very satisfying. Because *self-image* is commonly used to refer to a person's overall sense of self, using it to refer to parts of the self is confusing. The terms *true self* and *false self* are too limited. Federn's *ego states* suggests an ego separate from the states that is the "real person." In reality the "ego states" *are* the person.

Yet the word *role* is not entirely satisfactory either, because it draws attention to a general *idea* (such as son, protector, friend, etc.) and away from the fact that the role is filled by a *person*. The part-self is always a partial personality that fills a role in a particular and distinctive way.

I have come to call the roles that exist inside me "personality roles." The name is meant to highlight the fact that roles such as father, son and friend are pressed upon me by my relations with other people and made uniquely my own by my existing personality traits (which, of course, have been formed in the context of previous interactions with others). These traits make me a *particular* father, son or friend.

Coping with Trauma

When we experience traumatic events, the normal processing of memories into understood patterns and roles may be interrupted. The mind may simply refuse to "compute." For a while the memory may lie dormant and unprocessed.[10] The instinct to make sense of memories, however, is strong—so strong that a new personality dissociated from the structures of the main personality may appear in order to process the traumatic memory, keeping the main personality protected from it. This dissociated role then develops its own unique responses to and understanding of the world.

When I met Betty, she was thirteen different people. Inside her head we discovered a committee at war with itself. Some of her insiders were children, personalities that had split off in self-protection during sexual abuse over several years of her childhood. When she became a mother, her inside children would come out and play with her own children. Her kids thought all mothers had this skill. Other insiders were older and had well-defined personalities of their own. Some of them were kind, some were angry, some were dominant, some were retiring; but they all disliked and feared one another.

Betty discovered this crowd of inside people after becoming aware of blackouts that her neurologist was unable to explain or cure. A psychologist helped her to see that she had various personalities who were taking control of her body. When this happened, her actions and even her outward appearance changed. The seductive Betty Lou, for example, used different body language from the respectable young mother who occupied the same body. They also had separate memories, so that when Betty reemerged, she had no idea where she was or what she had most recently been doing.

Although all of this was strange and terrifying to Betty, she felt tremendously relieved to understand what was happening to her. She no longer felt crazy. As time went by, however, it became clear that she was not getting better. The angry insiders still fought each other for control of her body, often leading her into disastrous and shaming episodes. Hate and fear dominated her emotional life. Betty's disappointment over her lack of progress grew into alarm when one of the insiders took over and attempted suicide.

Betty did not begin to make significant progress until God unlocked memories of the mental, physical and sexual abuse she had suffered as a child—including horrifying recollections of being buried alive and of being forced to participate in satanic rituals involving rape and death. During the ritual abuse she had learned to escape by retiring deep within herself. Because this kind of abuse had happened many times, the adult Betty had split off several "children" to carry her unbearable pain.

As the Holy Spirit gently restored these memories, Betty slowly began to love the emotionally damaged children inside her. As they shared the terrible memories with her, she offered them comfort and acceptance, until one by one they merged with her. As aspects of herself that had long been separate reunited, Betty felt her personality expand.

The other insiders were older and more powerful. Jamie was a fierce, controlling person, a sergeant major who decided who would control the body at any given time. Betty Lou—the one who had made the desperate suicide attempt—was a promiscuous teenager who would go on drinking bouts. Some of the deadly insiders would carve satanic symbols on Betty's arms. It is easy to see why there was such deep dislike and fear between Betty and these others.

Betty's healing continued as she started to see that these insiders were also broken-off parts of herself. Much of her destructive behavior occurred because each insider, aware of the hatred of the others, was angrily or bitterly trying to take revenge. Actually Betty's insiders needed one another. The control that Betty Lou needed over her actions, for instance, was located in Jamie; the hard, controlling figure of Jamie, on the other hand, was cut off from the femininity of Betty Lou.

Although attaining cooperation and mutual dependence between the strong insiders was difficult, eventually they too began, somewhat grudgingly, to share memories at her therapist's encouragement. Eventually they actually began to appreciate each other's special abilities and to work cooperatively, yielding control to one another as the occasion required. In the end, they too merged.

Betty is still aware of distinct aspects within her own personality, but now she owns them herself. She can draw on Jamie's dominance, Betty Lou's femininity or whatever other roles she needs without blacking out and repressing memories. Above all, embodiments of different aspects of her personality no longer hate and fear one another. She is, at last, one whole person.

People like Betty are being discovered in surprising numbers. Many have developed multiple personalities to protect themselves from horrifying childhood memories of physical and sexual abuse—usually at the hand of a family member, and sometimes in the context of satanic rituals. Often children in this situation feel entirely powerless to cope in any other way. If they tell someone, will the adult perpetrator have to go to jail? What if no one believes them and they get punished for telling? For those caught in ritualistic abuse, the prospect of deliverance seems even dimmer: who will take seriously the accusation that satanic rituals are being performed on them by seemingly respectable adults?

It is important to remember that Betty and others who suffer from multiple-personality disorder are not as different from the rest of us as it might appear. Normal personalities also change personality roles to cope with different situations. Think about how we often talk of different sides of ourselves: "I'm not myself today"; "She's like a new person"; "I never knew he had it in him." The difference is that in the person with multiple personalities, childhood trauma has taken away his or her ability to move freely between roles at will. This person has lost the sense of unity between roles that the normal personality unconsciously takes for granted. In short, the normal personality never entirely loses its sense of "being me."

Normal personalities and multiple personalities, therefore, lie at opposite ends of one spectrum (see table 1). In between lie people who experience varying degrees of *dissociation* between personality roles.[11]

Normal Personality	Dissociated Personality	Multiple Personality
All memories are accessible to all personality roles.	An increasing number of memories are blocked off from some personality roles.	One personality role controls, while the others are unconscious; personality roles share few common memories.
All personality roles are unified by one will.	One will dominates most of the time, but personality roles are increasingly in conflict with one another.	All personality roles have independent wills; relationships between personality roles are often characterized by mutual hate and fear.
Body style between different personality roles varies only slightly.	Body style between personality roles shows increasing variation.	Body style between personality roles varies widely (for example, one personality role may be right-handed, another left-handed).

Table 1. The spectrum of dissociation

How Dissociation Starts

When strong dislikes arise between personality roles, a person begins to experience what we have been calling dissociation. In this situation the role that's in command most of the time finds it threatening to slip into a disliked role; it feels as if a power inside is taking over against the person's will, and she resists it. She becomes more aware of her internal divisions than the average person, and consciously or unconsciously she separates herself from a divided inner self. This separation, created in response to internal division, is *dissociation.*

I know this dynamic only too well. Having grown up under the influence of a dominant mother, I learned to obey her and developed a submissive personality role. In my teenage years a more assertive, masculine role developed in the context of other relationships. When I was relating to someone in this mode, I fiercely resisted the weakness of the passive role. Yet when I faced authority figures—especially if they were female—I found myself slipping back against my will into the submissive pattern.

This sense of being overcome by a powerful, opposing personality role is exactly what those trapped in compulsive behaviors experience. It makes sense, then, that compulsive behavior becomes increasingly common as we move across the spectrum of dissociation.

If the antipathy between personality roles becomes great enough because of trauma in childhood, the connections between them fracture altogether and multiple-personality disorder sets in. At this point the personality roles are at war; and like countries at war, they sever communication with each other, refusing for the most part to share memories. The will is now completely fractured into several wills, and the roles have become so distinct that we call them alternative personalities or "alters." The alters with the most assertive natures fight for control to assert their own dissociated will.

But why do strong dislikes between roles crop up in the first place? Does it take childhood abuse as extreme as Betty's to create such fear and self-distrust?

Although Betty's case is not as isolated as we would like to believe, dissociation more often begins under less extreme circumstances. Whenever a child finds herself in a relationship where one adult relates to her in two mutually opposed personality styles, she finds herself developing two mutually opposed personality roles in response. Take the child who grows up with an alcoholic father. She has to relate to two fathers—one drunk, the other sober. In response she develops several roles that conflict with one another. On one hand, she learns a people-pleasing role as she tries to be a "good girl" to placate the angry drunk. On the other, her more normal personality-part feels the injustice of the situation. Because fear of the father keeps this angry role suppressed, it begins to resent the dominant presence of the people-pleasing role; similarly the dominant role lives in fear that the angry role will break out. This situation produces the sense of an inner force driving the child (and later the adult child) to do something she does not want to do. In other words, it produces compulsive behavior.

Understandably, the person's conflicting roles and related compulsive behavior will tend to cause problems for her own children—whether she tries to bury the internal tensions she feels with drugs or alcohol or whether she simply suffers from violent, uncontrollable mood swings.

Not only alcoholics do this kind of damage to their children, of course. Any adult who experiences an uncomfortable amount of internal tension between personality roles may have the same effect. The more extreme the contrast between the personality roles that the adult presents to the child, the more extremely opposed the child's own roles will become. That's why victims of ritual abuse so often develop full-blown multiple-personality disorder. The process is clear from many therapists' experience with counselees as well as from my own work with people. In ritual abuse the child is typically forced to relate to an adult who first savagely abuses him or her and then displays affection. The dissonant roles the adult cultists display are calculated to produce as much conflict in the child as possible, so that he or she becomes emotionally vulnerable and subject to the cult's control. Perpetrators believe they can program split-off personalities to engage in cult activities.

Dissociation and Compulsive Behavior

I was not exaggerating when I described the struggle between conflicting personality roles as a war. Usually the repressed role doesn't like being repressed. This causes increasing internal tension. The dominant role grows to fear that the repressed part will break loose and destroy the life that she has worked so hard to build; the controlling role feels, in fact, as if she will die if she loses her dominance.

To keep the repressed role in its cage, the dominant role feels an overwhelming need to placate it. At this point compulsive behavior appears. The person ends up doing something that she sincerely hates doing; but the fear that the repressed inner self will get satisfaction by taking over entirely is so great that the person really feels as if she has no choice but to indulge that repressed role from time to time.

Consider a man implicitly or even explicitly taught as a child to be ashamed of his sexuality. He rejects his sexual self, which generates a life of its own. In time the adolescent becomes aware of his sexuality as a hostile personality role. He reacts to it by trying harder to suppress it; he is appalled that he has this "animal" inside. This continued suppression deepens the division and hostility still further.

Eventually the dominant role is forced to placate the hidden, sexual self in small ways to prevent it from becoming dominant. The man may feel overwhelmingly compelled to indulge his sexual self in masturbation or pornography or clandestine sex.

Sometimes dominant roles outwit their "prisoners" by placating them in a more morally or socially acceptable way. So the man who denies his sexuality might try to placate his sexual self with the sensual pleasure of eating. His resulting weight gain makes him feel less sexually attractive, which in turn reduces his temptation to act out sexually. The sexual self has been conquered! Or at least it seems so.

This scenario gets me thinking about pastors who get caught in sexual sin. Often they look like hypocrites, having ruthlessly condemned sexual immorality from the pulpit while indulging in it privately. How can they stand to live such dishonest lives?

The answer is fear—fear of the sexual "beast" locked up inside who must be placated occasionally to keep quiet. When the beast is privately given what he wants, the dominant personality role temporarily disappears in disgust. What the public sees in the pulpit is the controlling role railing against what it truly hates and fears—railing against it more vehemently, in fact, the more it hates and fears its repressed sexual role.

Sometimes the mutual hatred is taken out on the body itself, which is perceived as belonging to the hostile, suppressed role. In this light, otherwise inexplicable acts of self-mutilation, including eating disorders, make sense.

Summary: The Inner Conflict

The following points sum up what I have said so far about personality roles.

☐ Normal personalities play different roles that require them to draw on different sets of personality traits. These part-selves are called "personality roles" (or just "roles").

☐ Personality roles develop during childhood in response to other people, usually parents, who expect and reward specific behavior patterns.

☐ If one parent or two parents present the child with expectations that conflict with one another, the child will develop roles that exist in tension.

☐ The internal conflict between personality roles that dislike each other tends to deepen the dissociation between them and sharpen their separate identities.

☐ A disliked personality role can be suppressed as the leading role tries to deny it any outward expression. This leads to compulsive behavior; the suppressed personality role is placated by being allowed "out" occasionally.

☐ In the extreme case of deeply hostile personality roles resulting from trauma, the dissociation extends to separate memories and separate wills. This complete fragmentation of the self is called multiple-personality disorder.

What does personality-role fragmentation look like, and how can we begin to put the pieces of our selves back together? Two case studies in chapter three may help.

3
THREE FREDS
AND
TWO JANES

• • • • • • •

In this chapter *we're going to take a closer look* at two Christians I've counseled who fell somewhere in the center of the dissociation spectrum. Although neither had a full-blown case of multiple-personality disorder, each suffered much pain because of tensions between parts of his or her personality. To protect their confidentiality I have altered details; they have agreed to let me tell their stories in this way. They and I hope that the following analysis of their dissociated personality roles and the healing that came from reconciling them will help others who are trying to understand and change their own personality patterns.

In the case studies of Fred and Jane that follow, I not only distinguish between their personality roles but describe how I related to different roles differently. This is not as bizarre as it sounds. As I emphasized in the last chapter, each of us uses and relates to different roles daily as we relate to different people in different settings. The difference is one of degree: in most relationships we change roles more easily and unconsciously than either Fred and I or Jane and I were able to do, since their personality roles would suddenly reveal dramatically different sides of them.

In any event, I do not mean to imply that these roles were entirely separate personalities (as Betty's were in chapter two). Unlike people with multiple-personality disorder, Fred and Jane always knew when their "repressed selves" were taking over and making them act in ways they hated. Like many of us, they were painfully aware of their compulsive behavior and riddled with guilt for being unable to stop it.

The Perfect Politician

Fred was a brilliant, sensitive young man. But he had a problem. A secret problem.

Who could have guessed something was wrong? Fred was the kind of citizen any civic leader would praise. He volunteered time every week to work with deeply troubled inner-city teenagers, and because he was physically attractive and emotionally available, many kids responded to him. Often Fred found himself playing the role of surrogate father to these teens, trying to provide the support that their own fathers were unable or unwilling to give. Though the demands on his time became impossible, he was too compassionate to say no to someone in need.

Fred was also a successful politician who had won an important county office at an unusually early age. His speeches were powerful, his presence commanding: his deep voice, six-foot frame, striking red hair and intense blue eyes won people over. People were also attracted to the moral fervor with which he spoke as a deeply committed Christian. The crowds at each of his speeches grew larger because people wanted to hear him.

After each speech, however, Fred felt anything but successful.

In fact, he would fall into a black depression. He felt as if the crowds were responding to someone else—as if he were an actor playing a part. It seemed obvious to him that he was morally unfit for his position.

Though he often spoke about family values, personal responsibility and morality, he couldn't remember a time when he hadn't felt out of control of his own sex life. Before becoming a Christian he had pursued women as if they were trophies; once he had gotten what he wanted from them, he usually ended the relationship. Even after becoming a Christian Fred felt unable to sustain a relationship with a woman. Several times he fell wildly in love with someone he barely knew, then would find the romance had faded after two or three dates. Embarrassed, he would drop the woman abruptly. He was, in fact, terrified of women and found solace in pornography. He despised himself for doing so but couldn't seem to stop.

Why did he feel compelled to act this way?

As Fred and I talked about his patterns of relating to women, we began to realize that his problems started long before he became sexually active. The roots of his compulsive sex life and fear of intimate relationships lay in his childhood.

Fred's father had always been very self-centered, demanding that Fred provide him with emotional support and admiration rather than the reverse. When Fred failed at meeting all his father's emotional needs—no child could have succeeded at such a task—his father would punish him by withdrawing emotionally. Rarely was Fred rewarded when he did successfully boost his father's self-esteem. Fred's father never let his little son get close to him, nor did he respond warmly to his child's growing hero worship.

Fred's hunger for his father's love drove him to perform for him in many ways. Since his father often talked about sex and regarded women as playthings, Fred followed suit. His father actually enjoyed hearing details about Fred's sexual conquests, so

Fred brought home his experiences with his high-school girl-friends as if they were trophies.

Fred began to take control of this sick relationship with his father when he became a Christian at college. He found a male Christian leader who discipled him and loved him unconditionally as a friend. Unfortunately, though, Fred's hunger for approval was so deeply ingrained that even his best relationships were tinged by the need to perform. He was, at heart, a people-pleaser.

His legalistic church experience had only reinforced this tendency. There too, approval was carefully rationed out in response to performance. So on he went, driven toward the breaking point, incapable of forming normal friendships with women or men his own age. Lacking power over his personal life, he poured himself into a search for power in the political arena. The more power he gained in politics, however, the more frustrated he became with his inner weakness.

As a politician, Fred used his great abilities as a speaker to try to win approval. The approval never satisfied him, however, because it always seemed as if someone else were doing the speaking. Fred believed that if people knew what he was really like, they would despise him. He would alternate between hoping that just trying harder could win him the approval he craved and despairing that he would never feel acceptance. The emotional effort it took to keep performing was slowly destroying him.

Let's try to work out the pattern of roles that Fred had developed. We can then identify the conflict between roles that produced his compulsive people-pleasing behavior.

Fred the Performer. This was the politician who had the gift of public speaking and an acute insight into what people wanted to hear. He felt no emotion but acted as if he did. Fred's keen intelligence was put to use in this role.

Fred the Rescuer. This was the man who served as surrogate father to many young people. He responded deeply and emotionally to others' emotional needs. He had little wisdom to offer; he simply reacted when his button was pressed by a needy teenager.

Fred the Seducer. Made in his father's image, he had been trained to seduce women. This role was fiercely suppressed when Fred became a Christian. Fred's sexuality was located here, but not his intelligence, emotions or self-control.

The self-indulgent Seducer hated the Performer, whom he considered a puritanical tyrant. The Performer had taken to Christian legalism enthusiastically and was deeply embarrassed by the Seducer and his loose thoughts. This dislike, which was strongly returned, became a major source of inner tension. More than anything, the Performer feared losing control.

As the personality role most committed to following Christ, the Rescuer was disturbed by the other two roles' responses to people. On one hand, he constantly feared that the Seducer would take over and lead Fred into sin. Almost as bad was his struggle with the legalism of the Performer, whose insincerity deeply bothered him. These conflicts produced further inner tension.

When I first met Fred, his primary role was the Rescuer, while the Performer was an entirely rejected part of the self. That's why Fred could experience no joy at his political achievements. He thought of the Performer as another person and disliked his lack of sincerity.

Although the Rescuer couldn't say no to needy teenagers, he resented the impossible demands on his time. The lack of real affection he felt toward others caused a backlash; he would try to compensate for his lack of real intimacy with others by allowing the Seducer to take over for a while and indulge himself with a shallow romance or pornography. As soon as the need for intimacy was "medicated," the Seducer would be suppressed again. The romance would be dropped, the pornography put away.

After a while Fred found a new, more loving church and made friends with a Christian couple close to his own age. He began to experience unconditional acceptance in his new relationships.

With the help of a therapist, he also began to explore his inner tensions. (I will describe exactly how this worked in a later chapter.)

During our times together I came to know Fred's different sides and learned how to draw each one into a conversation. As each personality role came to trust me, I was able to talk to them about each other. My goal was to break down their mutual dislike and fear by acting as a trusted friend and intermediary for all of them.

Soon the Rescuer and the Performer saw their need of each other's characteristics. The intelligence and control of the Performer, for example, came to be resources that enabled the Rescuer to say no; eventually Fred was able to bring his time commitments under control. The Performer in turn learned about acceptance, forgiveness and expressing emotion from the Rescuer. They eventually merged to carry out Fred's public speaking, which became warmer and more emotional.

It was more difficult to persuade the Seducer to cooperate with the other two; returning his dislike, they also resisted at first. In time, however, they helped him understand that his sexuality was a good gift that had been abused, rather than an evil in itself. The Seducer needed these moral insights. He was also desperately in need of the warmth and emotional depth of the Rescuer to keep him from using people, as well as the self-control of the Performer to help him develop healthy, long-term relationships.

As I write this, Fred's process of healing is nearing completion. He has become better at knowing his own needs and controlling his own desires. He is still effective with the young people he helps, but is able to say no when he must. He is developing healthy relationships with women and even praying for a wife; for the first time in his life, the idea of long-term intimacy appeals to him. He enjoys his public speaking now and is getting even better at it.

The old names for his roles—Rescuer, Performer and Seducer—no longer fit. Control, Care and Playfulness are more accurate. Each takes control as the need arises, and they like one another. Fred is close to wholeness.

The Submissive Wife

In her husband Joe's absence, Jane could barely survive. Unable to cope with even the simplest chores, she would often take a whole day to carry out one small task. Joe, who loved her very deeply, was consistently gentle and supportive; he hired a housekeeper and generally tried to make her life manageable. His job often required him to travel, however, and I sometimes wondered if this was his way of escape.

A delicate woman in her mid-thirties, Jane had passed from one psychiatrist to the next in her search for help with depression and anxiety. Her current psychiatrist, who had been seeing her weekly for several years, had prescribed several different medications for her problems. The drugs flattened her mood so that she plodded through life with dull resignation. She had tried many different psychiatric drugs over the years, in fact, and eagerly took each new one offered. To these she added her own mixture of non-prescription medications, as well as still other medications prescribed by an internist for physical complaints. Afraid that she'd be unable to function if either physician cut back on her medications, she kept both of them ignorant of the other's treatments.

Jane's spirituality troubled her deeply. She felt guilty most of the time, worrying about her lack of faith and her past sins. She also constantly fought the temptation to become sexually immoral and leave her husband. As we prayed together over these problems, it became clear to me that she had a prayer life of great depth. I was perplexed, wondering how all these traits and experiences could coexist in one woman.

I was Jane's pastor, and my role was to assist her to grow spiritually, so I decided to focus on prayer during our times together. In her prayer life Jane was often conscious of spiritual attack and had learned to take authority over hostile evil forces.

Sometimes in my office she would pray silently over all her concerns while I prayed for her protection. I was always aware that her prayers seemed more profound (and more profoundly felt) than mine.

Jane had grown up in a very strict religious home; her parents were regarded as role models in their church. People knew nothing of the severe punishments they inflicted on Jane as a little girl. Any time she showed forcefulness, Jane's parents responded by beating and verbally berating her. Under this regimen Jane's forceful, energetic part went underground, leaving a passive, compliant Jane out to please her parents. Jane became a "good girl," submissive and dependent—a model daughter and a compliant wife. The forceful inner Jane, however, became more and more angry at her imprisonment.

In her teenage years the forceful self took control for a while; Jane referred to this as her "rebellious phase." This ended when she and Joe became Christians. Then once more the forceful Jane was imprisoned—this time with the help of prescription and nonprescription drugs. Jane was, in fact, internally repeating the kind of repression she had suffered at her parents' hands as a child.

As we met regularly to pray, "gentle Jane" came to trust me. With the help of the Holy Spirit we began to explore the inner terrain of her mind. (As with the case of Fred above, I will explain exactly how this worked in a later chapter.) One day we came into contact with her inner angry self, who suddenly emerged, taking over and spitting her anger out at me. This happened several times; my interaction with this personality role became more and more extensive.

At first this "forceful Jane" often behaved badly. She was streetwise and sassy, and her language left a lot to be desired. But I like teenagers and understand their anger, so it didn't bother me. To me this Jane was just another angry teen.

At first Jane was alarmed at the forceful Jane's emergence; but with my reassurance that her behavior would not be allowed to embarrass her or spoil her relationship with me, she cooperated. Eventually I made friends with the inner, angry Jane; her emergence became less abrupt and traumatic for Jane once she had gentle Jane's permission to come out. I rather liked this side of Jane's personality, but the contrast with the sweetly submissive Jane was a bit unsettling at times. Standing with her hands on her hips and feet wide apart, the forceful Jane once told me that the way to handle an awkward friend was to "kick her ass"—not exactly how the gentle Jane might view the situation!

Gradually the forceful Jane and I were able to talk about Jesus. Each time she emerged, gentle Jane listened in, and afterward she discussed how she felt about her other role. She began to show support for forceful Jane's growth.

Forceful Jane was changing too. She had revealed at first that she despised gentle Jane, calling her "hopeless" and complaining that "she never gets anything done." Soon, however, she began to accept my theory that gentle Jane was weak because she, forceful Jane, possessed all her drive and assertiveness. We explored together what the good qualities of gentle Jane were, and she came to see that these qualities (gentleness, sympathy and femininity) were the very things that she lacked.

Part of forceful Jane's contempt for gentle Jane was rooted in the knowledge that the latter kept her down with drugs. As gentle Jane began to see the need to cooperate with forceful Jane, she decreased her use of drugs, and the inner hostility lessened. Eventually Jane felt well enough to discontinue medication entirely; encouragingly, both sides of her were involved in the decision. For gentle Jane to do this took great courage. It marked a new level of trust in forceful Jane, for the drive and determination to change came from her.

One day forceful Jane admitted that she had come to respect her counterpart's spirituality. "When she prays, things happen," she told me.

"How do you feel about submitting to Jesus' lordship also?" I asked.

"I would like to," she said. For the first time forceful Jane and I prayed together. Quietly she accepted Christ's authority over her.

Gentle Jane was excited about this development. Up until this time Jane's Christian faith had repeatedly been sabotaged by forceful Jane's rebellion against authority. For the next few months gentle Jane began sharing her considerable knowledge of Christianity with her other personality role. Whole new vistas of faith opened up to her as she began to see how forceful Jane could help her experience a different side of the Christian life.

When strength and energy were needed, gentle Jane was now often trusting her counterpart to take over. At first this only happened during the day when Joe was at work, so he knew nothing of these changes. Because forceful Jane was still quite aggressive at this stage, I was concerned what Joe's reaction would be when they finally did meet.

One evening on a dinner date, forceful Jane emerged and suddenly began to argue with Joe. He didn't know what was happening. All he could see was that his passive, compliant wife had turned into a tiger. He did not enjoy the evening at all. Forceful Jane did not enjoy the date either; she made it clear, in fact, that she didn't like Joe. For some time afterward, both Janes decided that forceful Jane should stay inside when Joe was around.

Eventually Joe's continued patience with and kindness to Jane made an impression on forceful Jane, and she began to like him. She continued to stay out of sight in his presence, but watched him all the time.

A turning point came when gentle Jane was trying to understand her inability to respond sexually to her husband. During one of our discussions she realized that most of her sexuality was located in the forceful part of her personality. Forceful Jane, in turn, was excited by this realization, because it gave her a way of relating to her husband. "Now," she told me, "I know how to deal with him." The result was a dramatic improvement in their sex life, which helped Joe come to terms with other manifestations of the "forceful Jane" side of his wife.

He talked to me some months later. "I don't understand all that has happened," he admitted, "but Jane is a new person. She never seemed to be able to get anything done before, but now she has energy and ability. She can be as sweet as always, but now she seems stronger sometimes too. When I have to leave town I know she can cope. Our lives are better now."

At this writing the two Janes are closer together than ever, cooperating much like roles in a normal personality.

4

THE APOSTLE PAUL
LOOKS AT
PERSONALITY ROLES

• • • • • • •

Baruch Goldstein *was no ordinary doctor,* for no Jewish settler in the Kiryat Arba settlement outside Hebron in the Israeli-occupied West Bank can be ordinary. The settlement is a citadel of ultra-orthodox Judaism in the heart of aggressively held Palestinian territory. Nightly the cry goes up in the darkness around Kiryat Arba, "Death to the Jews!" Nightly the cry is flung back, matching passion to passion, hate with hate: "Death to the Palestinians!" The Jewish settlers stand on the fiery conviction that God gave them this land and they will not share it with Palestinians even if it means killing them all. They live in Old Testament orthodoxy, and the Torah is ruthlessly applied to everyone there through intense social pressure. There is no discussion, no democracy, just the rabbi's authority.

Goldstein became a hero in Kiryat Arba after he took an assault rifle and burst into a Palestinian crowd at the Tomb of the Patriarchs. Spraying bullets everywhere, he killed twenty-nine Palestinians before being shot himself. His grave at Kiryat Arba is revered as a martyr's tomb by Jews who regularly visit it.

If you want to understand Saul the Jewish, anti-Christian fanatic, then start with Baruch Goldstein. If you want to understand ancient Israeli society and its pressure to keep the law, start with Kiryat Arba.

Personality Division in Authoritarian Societies

Compulsive behavior is a basic human experience. No society can exist without some form of law. The very existence of such a law, however, immediately gives rise to an internal dissenting voice in the individual, demanding freedom and autonomy. At the same time society conditions the same individual toward submission with a powerful combination of rewards and threats. The more developed the ethics and laws of a society become, the more intense is the tension. If the society is also authoritarian, individuals feel pressured to divide their personalities into a law-keeping, submissive role and a rebel role—and to suppress the latter.

Since most ancient societies were authoritarian, this split was common in antiquity. The ancient Greeks and Romans discussed it in detail. Perhaps the clearest expression is from Ovid's *Metamorphoses:* "Desire persuades me one way, reason another. I see the better and approve it, but I follow the worse."

This statement stands in a solid line of tradition going all the way back to Euripides and expressed in many different variations in antiquity.[1] Such role tension was part of the apostle Paul's world, for he was raised in a famous university town, the Greek city of Tarsus. He was also raised as a Jew, and in this tradition too, with its fierce attachment to law-keeping, we find the familiar personality-role pattern of rebellion and submission.

The Rabbis and Personality Roles

The rabbis of Paul's time were well aware of the struggle between parts of the personality.[2] They used the Hebrew word *yetzer* for what I have called the personality role. The rabbis typically saw the division in the personality as a moral question, related to their law, the Torah. Human beings are born, they said, with an impulse to evil—the bad *yetzer*—which opposes the impulse to good—the good *yetzer*. The existence of the bad *yetzer* was their main explanation for sin. "It is thus primarily as the tempter within that the *yetzer ha-ra* [the bad *yetzer*] is represented in Jewish literature. Since it encompasses man's undoing by leading him into sin it is thought of as maliciously seeking his ruin, a kind of malevolent second personality."[3]

Yet the rabbis did not see the bad *yetzer* as intrinsically evil. Rather it was viewed like a willful child: likely to lean to the wrong, but not of itself wicked. Its leanings were said to include sexual desire and also the urge to dominate and compete. These are powerful urges, but not necessarily evil. G. F. Moore's *Judaism* explains:

> The impulses natural to man are not in themselves evil. When God looked upon the finished creation and saw that it was all very good [Genesis 1:31], the whole nature of man is included in this judgment, as R[abbi] Samuel ben Nahman observes: "And behold it was very good." This is the evil impulse! Is then the evil impulse *[yetzer]* good? Yet were it not for the evil impulse no man would build a house, nor marry a wife, nor beget children nor engage in trade.[4]

The rabbis recognized that the bad *yetzer* is a necessary part of the human personality. Like an unruly teenager, the bad *yetzer* rattled the orderly house of law that the rabbis were building, yet it could not be ejected.

So it was that with acute insight the rabbis developed a personality-role theory of their own. Their commitment to the law made them aware that there is resistance to the Torah in the human heart. The opposing will, the bad *yetzer*, resists the pressure to conform. It is a feisty rebel personality role. Yet there is something desirable about its energy, in spite of its opposition to the law.

The good *yetzer* was much less interesting to the rabbis, and they discussed it far less. It passively conforms to the demands of the law. This law personality role is recognizable as a part of the individual that seeks to please authority and submit to its demands. Its passivity is its flaw. It is no match for the energy of the rebellious bad *yetzer*. Part of the reason for its weakness is the fact that it does not come into being until the bar mitzvah ceremony, when the child becomes an adult. It is thus some thirteen years behind the evil *yetzer*, which starts at birth or earlier.

This division into bad and good *yetzers* is exactly what a personality-role approach would predict for people in a society where law is prized. Strong drives within the personality will always resist pressure to conform, and a normal person will respond by developing a people-pleasing, passive personality role that will conform to the law and a rebel personality role that will resist. It is predictable that sexuality and competitiveness will be located in the rebel role.

If the society applies enough pressure, the rebel role will be suppressed. This in turn leads to compulsive behavior by which the rebel personality role exacts its revenge. In the end, however, the good *yetzer* wins, for in the age to come the bad *yetzer* will be destroyed. Rabbi Judah teaches in the Talmud: "In the world to come God will bring the evil impulse [the bad *yetzer*] and slay it in the presence of the righteous and the wicked."[5]

In the meantime the battle between the good and bad *yetzers* goes on. In its weakness the good *yetzer* has one great resource—the law. In fact, the main battle for a pious Jew was to suppress the actions of the bad *yetzer* by means of the law that governed his whole life. It was the law that empowered the weaker good *yetzer* and made pious living possible under the law. So closely are the law and the good *yetzer* bound together that they come together into a young boy at thirteen when he becomes bar mitzvah—a son of the commandment. The rabbis observe that childhood is the time of development of the unruly rebel, the bad *yetzer*, while early adulthood sees the birth of the conforming role—the good *yetzer*. The transition comes when the law enters. From then on the bad *yetzer* is to be controlled and suppressed.

I have stressed that personality roles develop in response to relationships. In this light it is understandable that when the young Jew enters into the adult community of men, the role modeled on his father's obedience to the law comes to the fore. We should expect that the rebel role, which up to this point has been allowed freedom from the full rigor of the Torah, will protest.

Two responses to this situation are predictable. First, the sincere Jew will strive to totally suppress the rebel role. Since the latter cannot be destroyed, it will exact revenge in the form of occasional compulsive behavior. This moral failure before the law is very painful to the sincere believer, who tries still harder to suppress the inner tormentor, only to experience further defeat.

The covenanters of Qumran who wrote the Dead Sea Scrolls took this way of suppression. The heart cry of the struggler is captured in one of the scrolls: "I belong to wicked humanity, to the fellowship of sinful flesh."[6] We will find its echo in Paul's own writing in Romans 7, for this was his way too.

The second alternative offers a truce in the war between the personality roles, at the price of the law. The approval and other rewards that law-keeping brings in this society can be attained just as well through a technical obedience to the law. The Torah is reinterpreted to make obedience easier so that the rebel role can be placated without breaking the law. The believer then becomes a hypocrite who keeps the external form of the law but denies its spirit. This was Jesus' complaint against the Pharisees (Matthew 23:14).

Thus the war between the personality roles exactly matches the rabbis' observation of the struggle between the two *yetzers*.

Paul's Personality Roles

This was the rabbis' understanding of the law when Paul came to Jerusalem to study under Gamaliel. Now our task is to read back from the writings of the Christian apostle to uncover his mindset.

Like other Jews of his day, he experienced the inner tensions that go along with an attempt to obey the law wholeheartedly. The law role and the rebel role began their familiar battle. The question is, How did Paul deal with that rebel, the bad *yetzer?* Was it by modifying the law—the approach that Jesus criticized— or was it through a passionate, all-out struggle to kill the rebel personality role?

Paul seems to have known both.

> If anyone else thinks he has reasons to put confidence in the flesh, I have more: circumcised on the eighth day, of the people of Israel, of the tribe of Benjamin, a Hebrew of Hebrews; in regard to the law, a Pharisee; as for zeal, persecuting the church; as for legalistic righteousness, faultless. But whatever was to my profit I now consider loss for the sake of Christ. (Philippians 3:4-7)

Here Paul is harking back to his law role, looking back on his early life. The intense sense of privilege in his Jewish birth is clear. So too is his sense of having satisfied the law. This is possible only when we reduce the law to a set of actions and ignore the heart motivation. In Christ Paul has now learned a new way that enables him to see that this technical law-keeping was worthless. Did he see it at the time? Not in his law role. A law role maintains its illusions by splitting off all dissent and questioning into the rebel role.

Questions there had to be, for gentle Rabbi Gamaliel was willing to see that the Christians may have been right (Acts 5:34-39). Perhaps he knew of Jesus' insistence that the law requires pure motives and not just technical obedience. Gamaliel was Paul's teacher, so Paul would have heard about the discussion. But Paul was not open. Instead he seems to have suppressed the questioning voice in the way of a Pharisee, which he calls "the strictest sect of our religion" (Acts 26:5).

This is typical. Authoritarian societies always pressure their members to suppress their questions. It happens now in places like Kiryat Arba; it happened in Paul's society. Internal questioning cannot be tolerated, because the questions come from inside and feel disloyal. Of course the conflict is all the fault of the rebel role, as the submissive part of the self will declare: *If I listen to that voice, it will break loose and destroy everything that I have so carefully built.* Such struggles lead to passionate, even crazed attacks on the source of the questions. We try to suppress the voice within by silencing the voice without. If the external action is violent, then it also releases some of the anger of the suppressed role. In Goldstein's case, the Palestinians had to be removed. For Paul it was the Christians. Here's how Paul describes it:

> I too was convinced that I ought to do all that was possible to oppose the name of Jesus of Nazareth. And that is just what I did in Jerusalem. On the authority of the chief priests I put many of the saints in prison, and when they were put to death, I cast my vote against them. Many a time I went from one synagogue to another to have them punished, and I tried to force them to blaspheme. In my obsession against them, I even went to foreign cities to persecute them. (Acts 26:9-11)

Paul then goes on to describe the intervention of God.

> On one of these journeys I was going to Damascus with the authority and commission of the chief priests. About noon, O king, as I was on the road, I saw a light from heaven, brighter than the sun, blazing around me and my companions. We all fell to the ground, and I heard a voice saying to me in Aramaic,

"Saul, Saul, why do you persecute me? It is hard for you to kick against the goads."

Then I asked, "Who are you, Lord?"

"I am Jesus, whom you are persecuting," the Lord replied. (Acts 26:12-15)

The pious, law-keeping role was persecuting God! All its pretensions are unmasked. It stands revealed as a failure. What good now is its virtuous claim to have kept the law? How can it have kept the law when it opposed God himself? This is the stunning force of the vision. Jesus reveals and turns Paul's life upside-down forever.

The entire process of suppressing the voice within by the discipline of the law was mistaken. Even the law role cannot satisfy the law. This pious Jew was set free, then, to examine his motives and see that his very piety was leading him against God. The law system didn't work. All Paul's effort and discipline led only to pride of race, exclusiveness and self-righteousness, and God opposed them all. Paul was to go to the Gentiles (Acts 26:17-18)!

In the same stroke the true nature of the rebel side of his personality became clear. The rebel role was not purely evil, any more than the law role was entirely good. The bad *yetzer* could sometimes be good, and the good *yetzer* could sometimes lead to sin. So the law in the hands of the law role (the good *yetzer*) doesn't work. Trying to work for the victory of the good *yetzer* and the destruction of the evil *yetzer* by means of the law was a failure. Yet the entire system of Jewish law came down to this.

Law, Jewishness and Pride in Romans

There had to be a new way. This is the issue Paul faces in his greatest work, the letter to the Romans. In the seventh chapter in particular Paul brings into focus the law role's internal struggle to overcome the rebel role. Or as he would have said, he writes about the moment of disillusionment for the good *yetzer* as it faces its defeat and the failure of the law.

All through this chapter Paul writes of himself in the divided way that is characteristic of personality-role thinking. In verse 9 he says, "I died." Since he is alive and writing, he must mean that some other self has died. The sense of pain and inner struggle intensifies as he writes, "I do not understand what I do. For what I want to do I do not do, but what I hate I do" (v. 15). It would be hard to find a more precise statement of compulsive behavior; and here it is tied directly to a sense of internal division into two selves: "For I have the desire to do what is good, but I cannot carry it out. For what I do is not the good I want to do; no, the evil I do not want to do—this I keep on doing" (v. 19). It is very clear that the "I" who acts is separate from the "I" who wills.

Commenting on this passage, James Dunn writes, "[Paul] is confused by his powerlessness (v. 15) but he understands well enough that he himself is the subject of the actions that he himself abhors (vv. 15, 16). . . . That is why we must speak of a split in the 'I' rather than of a split between the 'I' and the flesh."[7]

Inevitably, when we discuss this passage we have a tendency to describe Paul's "I" as divided. The text itself presses it on us. That is why Romans 7 is a key passage for the understanding of personality roles in the Bible.

In the previous chapters Paul has been explaining the way of salvation through faith in Christ. He has contrasted it with a rival way of salvation offered by the Jewish rabbis who had been his colleagues in his days as an orthodox Jew. The Hebrews of Paul's time, like the Jews of Kiryat Arba today, regarded themselves with pride as God's chosen people whose great distinctive was the law of Moses. Keeping this law was an enormous privilege. The distinctive elements of the law, especially circumcision, marked Jews off from the rest of the world. Throughout the Roman Empire they lived together in their own quarters, sharing their distinctive food, clothing and lifestyle. Out of this developed the habit of despising the Gentiles which is evident in much Jewish writing of the time. Thus the humble sense of privilege in keeping the law all too easily became a feeling of racial superiority. As Paul remarks, "Now you, if you call yourself a Jew . . . rely on the law and brag about your relationship to God" (Romans 2:17). With this attitude any attempt to be a blessing to the Gentiles, as God intended in his covenant with Abraham, became impossible.

Jesus' critique of the Pharisees rested on a similar point: they despised the ordinary people. Instead of reaching out to share the covenant grace they had received, the Pharisees had turned inward in self-congratulation. In the process those Jews who did not keep the law strictly—the *am-ha-arets* or common people—were regarded as inferior. "Sinners," including tax collectors and prostitutes, were despised as being even lower than the common people and entirely excluded from the covenant. Jesus became notorious for reaching out to reincorporate them, even including some in his group of disciples.

The features of the law that marked Jewish exclusivity, notably circumcision, had become a trap that locked many Pharisees (including Paul himself in his early life) into ethnic pride instead of freeing them to appreciate God's grace for all. With this arrogance, all law-keeping lost its value, grace disappeared, and the Pharisees believed themselves to be worthy of God's choice. Driven by this self-righteous attitude, the Jewish leaders in the Gospels were all too ready to eliminate Jesus and to persecute Christians.

Paul believed, following Jesus, that the Jewish covenant ideal had degenerated into a legalistic sense of status and pride. When Paul, following the logic of Jesus, reached out to the Gentiles to bring them into the covenant, he too experienced persecution. As an ex-member of the persecuting oligarchy, Paul knew its psychology well—it was the psychology of the law role, or the "good" *yetzer,* which in its efforts to keep the law displays characteristic self-righteousness.

Paul's goal in Romans was to oppose this corrupted view of salvation and reclaim what he felt was the original way followed by Abraham, the way of faith. (This is his theme in Romans 4.) In the process he wished to open the door of the covenant to those rejected by Jewish exclusivism, the "sinners" of Israel and the despised Gentiles. He aimed to show that even the most godly in Israel were caught in sin and unable to fulfill the law: "We have already made the charge that Jews and Gentiles alike are all under sin" (Romans 3:9).

This radically undermined the Jewish exclusivism of the law role. Even the holiest Jew still needed the forgiveness that could come only through the sacrifice of Christ on the cross, Paul's theme in chapters 5—6. So the most obedient Jew found himself in the same needy place as the Gentiles and the "sinners" of Israel. The way of faith in Christ was the solution to the common problem of *all* the children of Adam. Unlike the rabbis' way, it was, and is, universal.

In Paul's systematic way, he turns next to the role of the law, which had become a means of establishing the Pharisees in pride and therefore in sin. Clearly a radical reevaluation of the law was in order, now that it had become clear that no one could keep it. What was the law for? Why did God give it?

Paul's answer is that it was given to expose human sinfulness. The Pharisees were not too strict; as Jesus showed, they were not strict enough. If they had viewed the law as God intended it, they would have seen that it condemned them. Instead of producing ethnic pride and superiority, it would have brought humility and solidarity with the Gentiles. Instead of separating Jews as children of Abraham who kept the law, it would have united them with the rest of the alienated children of Adam.

Into this state of universal need Paul brings the good news of forgiveness in Christ, received by faith. In the process of believing, people are lifted from the domain of the law's condemnation and set free to live a new way of freedom in the Spirit, the topic of Romans 8.

In Romans 7, then, Paul turns to the question, How could the law given by God have turned out so disastrously? His answer leads us into the anguish of the faithful Jew's experience, the war between the *yetzers* and the disastrous inability of the law to help the "good" *yetzer*. Behind the chapter lies Paul's memory of that moment on the Damascus Road when the "good" *yetzer* was exposed as God's opponent. Only in this context can Romans 7 be seen to fit consistently into the rest of the book.

In this chapter Paul aims to dispose once and for all of the question of the law in the old system. He is preparing ground for the revelation of the Holy Spirit as the basis of a new life, the topic of Romans 8. In subsequent chapters the law is rarely mentioned, because Paul here attains his objective. It only remains to explore the implication of all this for Israel as God's historic, chosen people (chapters 9—11). The practical section that concludes the letter (chapters 12—15) is Paul's statement of the new law of freedom, given in the light of Christ and the coming of the Spirit.

The Divided "I" in Romans 7

My discussion here will focus on verses 15-25. (Appendix 1 discusses the whole chapter in detail and addresses other views of this section.)

I do not understand what I do. For what I want to do I do not do, but what I hate I do. And if I do what I do not want to do, I agree that the law is good. As it is, it is no longer I myself who do it, but it is sin living in me. I know that nothing good lives in me, that is, in my sinful nature. For I have the desire to do what is good, but I cannot carry it out. For what I do is not the good I want to do; no, the evil I do not want to do— this I keep on doing. Now if I do what I do not want to do, it is no longer I who do it, but it is sin living in me that does it.

So I find this law at work: When I want to do good, evil is right there with me. For in my inner being I delight in God's law; but I see another law at work in the members of my body, waging war against the law of my mind and making me a prisoner of the law of sin at work within my members. What a wretched man I am! Who will rescue me from this body of death? Thanks be to God—through Jesus Christ our Lord!

So then, I myself in my mind am a slave to God's law, but in the sinful nature a slave to the law of sin. (Romans 7:15-25)

This description of a tragic situation plumbs great depths of despair. The pain is too real for us to treat this passage as a generalization of human existence, as some have tried to do. This is a human being in anguish of soul. The "I" must be taken at face value—this is Paul's own experience. What we have is two selves, or personality roles, at war with each other. The dominant religious role tries in vain to suppress the rebel role, and the usual compulsive behavior results. Dunn puts the situation well in an excellent modern commentary:

The explanation is, quite simply, that there is a split in the "I" here (v. 15) between my willing and my doing: "I don't do what I want, but I do what I hate." Although Paul rings the changes on the terms he uses over the next few verses, in order to give variety and not to press particular distinctions of meaning, the strength of feeling in the opening formulation should not be ignored; there are things he does which he abhors and detests, and yet it is he himself who does them. No wonder he opens his explanation with a confession of confusion or frustration: "I do not understand what I do, I do not even acknowledge my own action."[8]

Paul speaks as one caught helplessly between a desire for good and a rebellious will that overcomes that desire. No longer is "sin" the only villain; now it is "I" who "keep on doing" evil. Yet it is not the same I as the one who wills the good, but an inner opponent. Here is personality-role language at its plainest: the divided will in anguish over compulsive behavior.

This religious war is characteristic of those who most long for goodness, including faithful Jews. And this very longing encourages the split of the personality and the suppression of the rebel role. The compulsive behavior that results undermines the longed-for goodness. It is the human tragedy that a desire for goodness should lead to such hopelessness and despair.

In another mood, of course, the "good" self can feel victory, but only at the price of softening the internal demand of the law, as Jesus often pointed out to the Pharisees. This "victory" leads immediately to pride and exclusivism, as we saw above. Such is the characteristic problem of the "good" or religious self.

The conclusion is inescapable: Romans 7 is not about war between the flesh and the Spirit in the human heart, as many commentators have argued. Rather it describes a struggle entirely inside the old nature, which contains both a religious will to do good, defined by the law, and a will to oppose it (see figure 1).

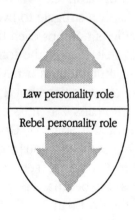

Figure 1. The war between personality roles in the religious person without Christ

There is a war between selves in the religious person who is not a Christian, an internal struggle all the more painful because it is hopeless. It goes on in the absence of new life in Christ.

Romans 7 reflects pre-Christian experience. This is the war between the *yetzers* so familiar to the rabbis, with one essential difference: the law and the "good" *yetzer* lose. Paul is not describing the war between the old life of flesh and the new life in the Spirit. That will come in the next chapter. Romans 7 pictures the struggle inside the old fleshly nature, betraying its internal division. Dunn's commentary almost reaches this conclusion, but then draws back: "The 'I' is split . . . and it is not the split itself that sin uses, as though sin could manipulate both I's to achieve a kind of schizophrenia."[9] Actually, that is exactly what is happening. *Schizophrenia,* literally a divided mind, is a very precise summary of the passage. (Of course, neither Dunn nor I intend to imply the technical sense of schizophrenia as a mental illness.)

On the other hand, the passage also applies to the Christian. The flesh nature does not disappear when one becomes a believer, so there is inevitably a struggle to live in the Spirit rather than the flesh. That battle is not, however, the battle of Romans 7, but of Romans 8. In that chapter the tone is quite different. The struggle is present, but there is a new confidence in the possibility of victory—not a certainty, but a real possibility. The hopeless frustration of Romans 7 is missing entirely. The new factor is the presence of the Spirit of God, and this is what distinguishes the longing of the religious soul of Romans 7 from the believer's conflict in Romans 8 (see figure 2). Victory over besetting sin is now possible because the Spirit is supporting the newly reborn spirit of the Christian. Yet this does not mean that we cease to be engaged in the flesh with its old internecine warfare.

The Christian, then, has a double battle: (1) the war between opposing parts of the self—the personality-role struggle (Romans 7), and (2) the struggle between the renewed self aligned with the Spirit on one hand, and the entire old self or flesh nature. This battle is different and is the subject of Romans 8.

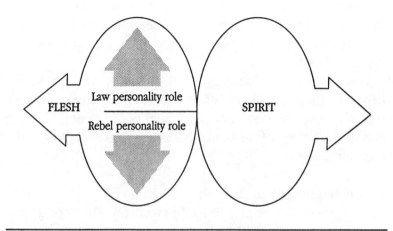

Figure 2. The double battle in the Christian's life

The old struggle between personality roles goes on in the flesh (left) within the larger war between the flesh and the Spirit.

The first struggle always continues, even after a person becomes a believer. It is often neglected, though, because it lies within the boundary of the old nature still remaining in the Christian's life. The commentators are correct: Romans 7 *is* about a Christian's struggle. The difference is that it is a warfare against compulsive behavior, waged entirely *within the flesh* or old nature. It is nonetheless real, as we have seen throughout this book. It is the same war experienced by sincere non-Christians. The conflict in Romans 8 is a different story, an exclusively Christian struggle between the flesh and the Spirit.

Being aware of the lower-level battle changes the meaning of the Christian's struggle. The easy triumphalism that assumes all problems of compulsive behavior are solved when one becomes a Christian is false. The lower-level war between personality roles can continue in the Christian soul too. We still live in the "old epoch"; we still wrestle with the flesh—it has not disappeared. Precisely because it has not disappeared, its internal struggles continue. There is a warfare *inside* this domain of the flesh, and since this domain continues in existence for the Christian, the old struggle continues as a civil war between the parts of the flesh. This war continues alongside the greater war waged between flesh and Spirit.

This is why Christians struggle with old patterns of compulsive behavior. They faced them before becoming Christians, and they still face them afterward. Romans 7 applies to the non-Christian part of the believer (the flesh) just as much as it applies to the non-Christian.

A New Beginning in the Spirit

This exposes another part of Paul's argument. The "good" part that wanted to keep the law, Paul says, had its own characteristic sins. Rigorous attempts to keep the law often led to the sins of pride and exclusivity. Thus even the "good" personality role offers no hope for righteousness. And this explains why the answer to the war of Romans 7 is not the death of the opposing personality role, as the religious person expects, but rather the fresh start in the Spirit described in Romans 8. Only in this way can we explain the transition from chapter 7 to chapter 8:

There is now no condemnation for those who are in Christ Jesus, because through Christ Jesus the law of the Spirit of life set me free from the law of sin and death. For what the law was powerless to do in that it was weakened by the sinful nature, God did by sending his own Son in the likeness of sinful man to be a sin offering. And so he condemned sin in sinful man, in order that the righteous requirements of the law might be fully met in us, who do not live according to the sinful nature but according to the Spirit.

Those who live according to the sinful nature have their minds set on what that nature desires; but those who live in accordance with the Spirit have their minds set on what the Spirit desires. The mind of sinful man is death, but the mind controlled by the Spirit is life and peace; the sinful mind is hostile to God. It does not submit to God's law, nor can it do so. Those controlled by the sinful nature cannot please God.

You, however, are controlled not by the sinful nature but by the Spirit, if the Spirit of God lives in you. And if anyone does not have the Spirit of Christ, he does not belong to Christ. But if Christ is in you, your body is dead because of sin, yet your spirit is alive because of righteousness. And if the Spirit of him who raised Jesus from the dead is living in you, he who raised Christ from the dead will also give life to your mortal bodies through his Spirit, who lives in you.

Therefore, brothers, we have an obligation—but it is not to the sinful nature, to live according to it. For if you live according to the sinful nature, you will die; but if by the Spirit you put to death the misdeeds of the body, you will live, because those who are led by the Spirit of God are sons of God For you did not receive a spirit that makes you a slave again to fear, but you received the Spirit of sonship. And by him we cry, "*Abba,* Father." The Spirit himself testifies with our spirit that we are God's children. (Romans 8:1-16)

This completes the transition from a struggle entirely within the flesh to a higher-level struggle between the old life of the flesh and the new life in the Spirit. As the Spirit rebuilds more and more of the person into the new life, the struggles of the old life are reduced. The reign of Christ extends in the Christian's life as sanctification continues.

This doesn't happen inside the domain of the flesh, where the law condemns. Instead, that domain shrinks. The old battle between the personality roles or *yetzers* continues as intensely as ever, but in a smaller and smaller territory. That is the lesson of Romans 8, which contrasts the slavery of 7:14-24 with the assertion of 8:14: "those who are led by the Spirit of God are sons of God." Only by becoming "the new man" can one reach the calmer waters of Romans 8 and the new battle in which we are free of "obligation . . . to the sinful nature" (8:12).

The two battles are linked by the process of sanctification. Exactly how this new self, aligned with the Spirit, interacts with the old broken life with its personality-role warfare remains to be seen in my next chapter.

The sheer brokenness that sin causes is graphically seen in the personality-role war and the compulsive behavior that goes with it. Here is the human soul in anguish, caught in a deadly trap, longing for goodness, only to be defeated by the rebel role on one hand and its own tendency toward self-righteousness on the other. This is Paul's point in Romans 7.

A personality-role approach to psychology, then, is consistent with the apostle Paul's view of himself. Of course his exploration of the self is expressed in religious terminology and uses the cultural ideas of *yetzer*. Even so, his conclusions are consistent with the approach I have outlined in the earlier chapters of this book.

5

SELF AND THE CHRISTIAN

• • • • • • •

At this point *it might seem as if a harmonious* relationship between your personality roles is all you need for happiness. But that is not the case. Internal conflicts are bad, as we have seen, and resolving them is good, but a further step is needed. After all, a person could be unified and yet remain selfish and wicked.

Reducing internal conflicts is worthwhile and promotes health in the personality. But health is quite separate from goodness. A very evil person could still be healthy in body and mind. The distinction between health and goodness is vital, for if we confuse the two we end up with salvation by psychology. The proper aim of psychology is mental health, not the soul's salvation. But in our day, when "feeling good" is many people's principal aim in life, psychology is frequently expected to produce happiness and fulfillment. Sometimes secular therapists encourage this, stepping beyond their appropriate role and becoming practitioners of "psychoreligion."

Like all sciences, psychology makes sense only within an external framework of values. This framework comes from religion.

In Christianity a healthy mind, like a healthy body, is very desirable. So Christians should be pleased when therapists help people toward better mental health. But Christianity teaches that there are other, more important values. Chief among them is goodness. Even after you have gained peace between your personality roles, you remain as far from that goal as before.

We have seen Paul struggling with the inner tensions between personality roles in Romans 7. His solution is not inner unity, but a relationship with God as defined in Romans 8. This new relationship with God does not solve the inner tensions, but it changes them. A new element has been introduced, the indwelling Spirit of God. The tensions continue, but they now include the war between "the flesh" and the Spirit.

Just as it is inappropriate for psychotherapists to offer salvation, it is wrong for Christians to suppose that Christian faith produces mental health. Throughout this book I describe the ongoing struggles of Christians. The "happily ever after" idea is not part of authentic Christianity as we experience it on earth. It belongs to heaven.

In the struggle for a holy life, however, a unified mind is an important help. It reduces confusion and helps us to "will one thing." It is important to be able to choose holiness with my whole self. That is why I have been addressing the psychological issue of unity of the will.

Introducing the Flesh

Now that we understand the inner tensions, we can avoid a common mistake. The war between the flesh and the Spirit is not the same conflict as that between personality roles. The war between personality roles in Romans 7 is the struggle for mastery between the parts of my old nature. The battle between my flesh and the Spirit is a struggle between the entire self-based system of the old me and the new system built around my relationship with God.

That's why it would be wrong to identify any single personality role as "the flesh." There is a strong tendency to do this, especially when we are suppressing a hated personality role that drags us into compulsive sinful behavior. We want to reject it. Yet we cannot eliminate the offending personality role, for it is a part of our self. It has to be rehabilitated. Trying to "crucify the flesh" by eliminating any personality role is doomed to failure.

This was Martin Luther's great discovery. For years this monk tried to destroy the boisterous, fun-loving part of himself. He whipped himself and starved himself, but the part he so disliked refused to die. The trouble was that his religious role, which was so busily trying to kill off "the flesh," was itself part of the flesh. The problem is the same as that of the young woman who, hating her own sexuality, tries to kill it off by anorectic fasting. She cannot succeed in killing part of herself. It's a case of all or neither.

What does Paul mean then by "the flesh"? The clearest answer I know comes from Donald Guthrie: "The flesh is myself seeking its own ends in opposition to the Spirit of God. . . . *Sarx* [flesh], ethically conceived, is human nature, man viewed in his entirety apart from and in contrast with the righteousness and holiness of God."[1]

When my life goal is to satisfy myself, I am "in the flesh." Apart from God, no other way of life is ultimately possible. If my role tensions are unresolved, I pursue a variety of self-goals; if I have reached unity, I pursue a single self-goal. Either way the goal is self-oriented rather than submitted to God. Therefore *all* my roles participate in the pursuit of self-satisfaction, and *all* are part of "the flesh."

Figure 3. The human being in the flesh
The self with personality roles in mutual opposition, represented by arrows pointing in different directions. The spiritual dimension is up out of the plane of the page. These personality roles play no part in that dimension.

In Romans 7 it is very striking that one role pursues the law while another opposes it. Yet the solution is not, as we might expect, to eliminate the opposing role. Instead the indwelling Spirit draws the *entire* personality toward God, including both roles. This new orientation of the person is called being "in the Spirit." It is opposed by the old tendency to focus on self-interest (selfishness), which is being "in the flesh."

The point of personality-role study is now clear. As long as I am apart from God, it makes no difference spiritually whether I am dissociated into opposing roles or not. Once I am in relationship with God, though, personality roles have the potential to unite around the Spirit within. So my pursuit of inner harmony becomes part of my pursuit of holiness.

A divided self can pursue God's will only partially, against internal opposition. Paul calls such a person "the fleshly man" *(sarkinos)*. The unified person who seeks God's will wholly is called "the spiritual man" (*pneumatikos,* from *pneuma,* "spirit"). The person who is not seeking to submit to God at all is called "the natural man" (literally, the *soulish* man, *psychikos*). Such people play no part in the realm of spiritual things, for they are not indwelt by the Holy Spirit, and their own spirit is dead. They are limited to relating to other people through their roles (that is, their soul). They are incapable of relating to God.

The man without the Spirit [the natural man, *psychikos*] does not accept the things that come from the Spirit of God, for they are foolishness to him, and he cannot understand them, because they are spiritually discerned. The spiritual man *[pneumatikos]* makes judgments about all things, but he himself is not subject to any man's judgment:

"For who has known the mind of the Lord
that he may instruct him?"

But we have the mind of Christ.

Brothers, I could not address you as spiritual but as worldly [literally "fleshly," *sarkinos*]—mere infants in Christ. (1 Corinthians 2:14—3:1)

To put the flesh to death is to focus my whole being on God's will, submitting gladly to his authority as the center of my life. This new life involves a relationship between my human spirit, newly made alive by God, and his Holy Spirit inside me.

The New Creature

Every role is called out by a relationship, as I showed in chapter two. I start as a child with the roles created in me in response to my parents. And when I first encounter my heavenly Father, it is natural that I will try to relate to him through one of my existing roles, often the one formed in response to my earthly father. Unfortunately, this role was in some degree a response to my father's sinfulness. And this is true even if my experience of my father was positive. My father was sinful, like all people, and so the personality role he called out in me adapts to his sinfulness as well as to his good features.

If I try to relate to God as I relate to my earthly father, I end up projecting my father's failings onto my heavenly Father. This can be very damaging. For example, it is hard for those who were once abused by their father to relate to God as Father. They tend to see God as angry or demanding or remote. For most of us things are not as bad as this, but the problem remains. We have a flawed image of God derived from a human and therefore sinful father, so we have developed a role with a flawed response to him. This damaged personality role is simply not adequate to relate to God.

What happens when God draws me into a relationship with himself? The Bible's answer is clear: I become "a new creation" (2 Corinthians 5:17). Just as my earthly father called out one of my earliest roles, so now my heavenly Father calls out a new role. This new part of my personality is, in Jesus' words, "born of the Spirit" (John 3:8).

Here is the miracle of new birth. A relationship with God is like no other relationship, for God is pure Spirit. He created us with a special capacity to relate to him in the life of the spirit. We are made in the image of God—that is what makes us human. This is another reason our relationship with God demands a new kind of personality role. A soul personality role relates to the world of humankind. A spirit personality role is necessary if we are to relate to God.

The dormant capacity to relate to God awakes to life at his call and becomes the center of a new role. I become truly a *new* creature. There really is a new me at the center of my being, existing in intimacy with the newly indwelling Spirit of God. I come alive spiritually. The Bible calls this new personality role my "spirit." This does not mean that I *have* a spirit, but rather that I *am* a spirit. The spirit is me in relationship with God. That is precisely what personality-role language describes.

When the Bible describes us as humans interacting in the world, it calls us "souls," or "soulish" persons. This is usually translated "natural man." Once again, it is not that I *have* a soul, but that I *am* a soul. The soul is me in relationship with other people. My soul, this me-in-relationships, is the set of roles that make up my personality. Thus the personality-role language developed in my previous chapters serves as an effective bridge between the Bible and the insights of psychology. I *am* my roles, and when I relate to people, the various roles correspond to the soul.

The role called forth by God, however, is my spirit. It is qualitatively different from the roles that make up my soul. In this role I exist in relationship with God, who is Spirit. The new birth is the birth of this new role. It is a new start to a new life. It is in truth a "new creation."

The War Between the Flesh and the Spirit

The Bible describes spiritual growth as the process of making us holy. The essence of the process is that we are made more like Jesus. Personality-role language makes this easy to understand. At the center of the Christian's life is the human spirit, newly alive, in intimate communion with the indwelling Holy Spirit of God. The spirit role, like most roles, reflects its source. Because God calls it out, it reflects his nature as I respond to him and learn to relate to him.

This new role disrupts the previous self-focus of the old personality roles already present, so there is great tension between these old personality roles and the new spirit role. This tension is resolved by the Holy Spirit as he brings each personality role under the rule of Christ. That is growth in holiness. As each role submits to Christ's lordship, new behavior flows out.

As I emphasized above, it is a grave mistake to try to suppress or kill my old personality roles. They are part of my memory; they do not die as long as I am alive. Instead they are to be brought under the rule of Jesus. As the Bible puts it:

Therefore, I urge you, brothers, in view of God's mercy, to offer your bodies as living sacrifices, holy and pleasing to God—this is your spiritual act of worship. Do not conform any longer to the pattern of this world, but be transformed by the renewing of your mind. Then you will be able to test and approve what God's will is—his good, pleasing and perfect will. (Romans 12:1-2)

At the start of the Christian life, the roles exist in a self-centered structure through which I relate to others, as we have seen (figure 3 above). Then God in sovereign grace creates the new me, and the spirit role arrives together with the Holy Spirit. This is somewhat similar to the rabbis' doctrine of the partnership between the good *yetzer* and the law, as outlined in chapter four. But there are two important differences. The first is that the feeble good *yetzer* is part of my old human nature, while the spirit role is a new creation. Even more significant is the replacement of the law with the mighty Spirit of God. These differences propel us from the disillusionment of Romans 7 to the new realm of Romans 8.

The arrival of the Spirit of God makes me a Christian. It is not that some single personality role in the old, natural self becomes a Christian. The roles are incapable of relating to God. When they try, they end up with human religion and we are back in Romans 7. Only the spirit role can relate to God.

Christian therapists working with people who have multiple personalities sometimes try to lead the different "alters" to faith in Christ. This cannot work, for a partial person cannot become a whole Christian. What we *can* do, if the person is already a Christian, is to recognize the existence of the living spirit of the person in intimacy with the Spirit of God within. Then we can bring the alters into harmony with their own spirit and into submission to the Holy Spirit.

What is true of the alters in a multiple personality is equally true of the personality roles in a more normal person. They constitute the natural part of us with which we relate to the world of people. They are inadequate to relate to God.

When we are made new creatures, our inner structure is radically changed. The new spirit role, teamed with the Holy Spirit, intrudes into the battlefield of the soul's roles. Their presence introduces a whole new realm of conflict. The personality roles may fight between themselves for mastery, but these are mere skirmishes compared with the battle in which every soul role fights against the spirit role. This is the war between the spirit and the self-oriented soul, which we call the flesh.

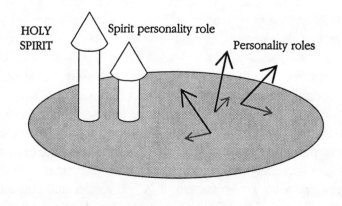

Figure 4. The process of spiritual growth
The Christian person indwelt by the Holy Spirit and with the new spirit role aligned alongside. The old personality roles (see figure 3) are slowly being brought into alignment with the spirit role (toward the vertical).

Growing in Holiness

The main work of the Spirit of God within the believer is to bring the scattered roles that make up the personality into harmony with the person's spirit under the lordship of Jesus. The Christian looks like figure 4. Not only are the old roles opposed to one another, but they all also oppose the new spirit role. Under the influence of the Spirit of God, each role in turn is being brought into alignment. Once again, this is Paul's description of the process:

> Those who live according to the sinful nature have their minds set on what that nature desires; but those who live in accord-

71

ance with the Spirit have their minds set on what the Spirit desires. The mind of sinful man is death, but the mind controlled by the Spirit is life and peace; the sinful mind is hostile to God. It does not submit to God's law, nor can it do so. Those controlled by the sinful nature cannot please God.

You, however, are controlled not by the sinful nature but by the Spirit, if the Spirit of God lives in you. And if anyone does not have the Spirit of Christ, he does not belong to Christ. But if Christ is in you, your body is dead because of sin, yet your spirit is alive because of righteousness. And if the Spirit of him who raised Jesus from the dead is living in you, he who raised Christ from the dead will also give life to your mortal bodies through his Spirit, who lives in you. (Romans 8:5-11)

Do not conform any longer to the pattern of this world, but be transformed by the renewing of your mind. (Romans 12:2) As this process of sanctification proceeds, the structure of mutual hostility and accommodation between the old personality roles is replaced with a new pattern. It is like a man building a new home in the middle of his old house. One day he digs up the living-room floor and lays the start of a new foundation. Day by day he adds to the new structure, using the old as raw material. The old house was made up of conflicting styles—a classical entrance, one window modern and straight while another was gilded and ornate, a gothic roof, brick walls mixed with stucco, and so on. As these enter the new structure, they all change, and the old conflicts are transformed by the master builder into a new and beautiful harmony. Bit by bit the new house consumes the old as the new foundation and walls extend. Soon the old house is a ruin, a setting for the exquisite home rising within it. One day the old, mixed-up house will be gone, and all that will be left is the new home. The old house will be dead, yet its parts will live on in the new (again, see figure 4).

This parable is a picture of the death of the old person and its replacement with the new creature. It illustrates the way the old conflicted structure of personality roles is reconstituted into the new creature: "You were taught, with regard to your former way of life, to put off your old self, which is being corrupted by its deceitful desires; to be made new in the attitude of your minds; and to put on the new self, created to be like God in true righteousness and holiness" (Ephesians 4:22-24).

The Christian retains the characteristics of the old personality, its roles. They are the raw materials of the new person he or she now is. They are arranged in a new personality structure, however, focused on God rather than self. This does not happen instantaneously; it is a process. It starts at a definite point, and it ends at heaven's gate.

Here again Martin Luther is a good illustration. In his ongoing attempt to kill off the old boisterous role with painful penance, he crawled up the steps of a church in Rome on his knees. Then his eyes were opened, and he saw that those who have been justified should live by faith. His spirit was reborn from above. Over the years that followed, Luther learned to know God through faith rather than works. He gave up trying to kill his boisterous self, and it too came under the rule of Christ. Neither side died; instead they were *both* transformed. But the old tormented, self-oriented structure that was Martin Luther—that died.

Of course it took time for the two parts to learn their new ways. The old ascetic Martin would break out now and again, usually during debates. And the old boisterous Martin, rejoicing in his new freedom in Christ, fell in love with a nun, happily married her and raised a host of noisy children. He had truly found himself in Christ! Of course the old Martin could break out here too, usually in coarse language, but as always the new peace in the Spirit was unmistakable: he really was growing.

As our personality roles begin to "conform to Christ," behavior starts to change. The spirit role relates to God, not to the world of people. Relating to people is the function of the soul roles, which act as intermediaries between the spirit role and the world of people. So as our soul roles cooperate more and more with our spirit role, our behavior becomes more and more Christlike.

Christian growth, then involves the development of all parts of my personality—all my roles—into harmony with the Spirit. This is why suppression of a disliked personality role will not help toward holiness of life. *All* my roles must be brought under the rule of Christ. Eliminating hostility between opposing roles is a necessary part of growth in holiness.

The unifying effect of good therapy becomes a contribution to my spiritual growth if the soul roles are united around the spirit role in submission to Christ. In practice, each area of my life and my relationships is transformed by God. Over the years, the angry me learns to be strong without hatred, and the people-pleasing me learns to serve selflessly. These are the struggles of Christian growth. They are what this book is about. Personality-role thinking is helpful in clarifying the process. But the work of doing it in cooperation with God's Spirit is, as always, hard work.

Continue to work out your salvation with fear and trembling, for it is God who works in you to will and to act according to his good purpose. (Philippians 2:12-13)

The Roles of God

The normal personality contains personality roles; such roles are not the exclusive property of dysfunctional persons. Recall the spectrum of table 1, for example, which shows that dysfunction comes not from the *existence* of personality roles but from *tension* between them.

The ability to play roles is part of the normal person's equipment for living with others. It develops in the community life of the home and is a normal part of growing up. Jesus is the only fully "normal" person who lived, and he shows clear evidence of personality roles. One moment he is lambasting the Pharisees with sledgehammer words designed to break through their hardened hearts, the next moment he tenderly holds a child in his arms. The beauty of Jesus' personality is that he switches so readily and naturally between these contrasting roles. Obviously there is no tension between them at all. (Remember, it is not having personality roles that is dysfunctional, but their mutual fear and dislike.) Jesus' will is unified, and all the roles work in harmony—that is true normalcy.

Since human beings are made in the image of God, the human personality is the surest model we have of God's nature. Augustine suggested this approach as a means of understanding the Trinity, and Millard J. Erickson takes up the idea in his *Christian Theology:*

In seeking for thought forms or for a conceptual basis on which to develop a doctrine of the Trinity, we have found the realm of individual and social relationships to be a more fruitful source than is the realm of physical objects. This is true for two reasons. The first is that God himself is spirit; the social and personal domain is, then, closer to God's basic nature than is the realm of material objects. The second is that there is greater interest today in human and social subjects than in the physical universe.

As a self-conscious person, I may engage in internal dialogue with myself. I may take different positions and interact with myself. I may even engage in a debate with myself. Furthermore, I am a complex human person with multiple roles and responsibilities in dynamic interplay with one another. As I consider what I should do in a given situation, the husband, the father, the seminary professor, and the United States citizen that together constitute me, may mutually inform one another.

One problem with this analogy is that in human experience it is most clearly seen in situations where there is tension or competition, rather than harmony, between the individual's various positions and roles. The discipline of abnormal psychology affords us with extreme examples of virtual warfare between the constituent elements of the human personality.

But in God, by contrast, there are always perfect harmony, communication, and love.[2]

Evidently personality roles are known in theology as well as in psychology and literature. Here is a second illustration:

If in respect to spiritual being God is one, in what respects is God diverse or multiple? We have already seen diversity of attributes, emotions, purposes and actions. Is there sufficient evidence to add diversity in another respect, that of persons? Could the one underlying common psyche (the unconscious) have three distinguishable centers of consciousness? Like an ocean (of one substance) with three waves (modes of its existence), does the one personal, spiritual Being subsist in three personal modes?[3]

Christian thinking about the Trinity has settled over the centuries into a series of statements that any new approach must affirm if it is to be considered orthodox. The first of these statements is the most fundamental: *God is one.* We do not worship three gods in the persons of Father, Son and Spirit; we worship one God, the upholder and creator of the universe. This is the fundamental statement of the Old Testament, the Jewish Bible.

The second statement is *Jesus is truly God.* This requires us to avoid placing Jesus on a lower level of being than the Father. In terms of being or essence, Jesus is equal to the Father. (Jesus is also "truly man," but that leads us into another area of Christian truth.)

Any model of the Trinity must attempt to bridge the logical gap between these two fundamental statements, helping us to understand how they fit together. A model like modalism—that the one God acts in different ways or modes—does justice to the first statement but falls short on the second. A model like tritheism—the worship of three gods—flatly contradicts the first fundamental statement. Thus we use the two statements, together with a statement specifying the deity of the person of the Holy Spirit, as tests that must be passed by any model of the Trinity.

How does the personality-role model come out in this test? The first statement, the unity of God, is basic to the model. No one disputes that a person is a single being, so the idea of God as a personal being has always led directly to the affirmation of the first truth. When we affirm that God is personal, we simultaneously affirm that God is one.

The heart of the problem of the Trinity is reconciling the idea of a personal God with the notion that the person we know as Jesus Christ is also truly God. Jesus revealed himself as divine, but he also displayed an intensely personal relationship with the Father, who is truly God. So while Jesus is truly God, there is more to God than Jesus alone.

The classical answer is to say that God reveals himself in three persons, Father, Son and Spirit. This immediately presents a problem: how can three persons be said to be one? The classical model proposes that they are one because they consist of the same material. In a similar way a family is one, sharing the same flesh and blood. So God is thought of as a spirit "substance" at the deepest level of being, and this spirit substance is shared by the three persons of the Godhead.

The classical model has always had problems. It places the essence of the Godhead in a substance rather than in a person, so that it becomes difficult to speak of God in his entirety as "he." Such personal language is more appropriate to the personal realm, but there God is three, so that "they" would be normal. Indeed the biblical name of God in the Hebrew is Elohim, which is a plural form. Still, it seems unsatisfactory that God's essence should be a substance rather than personality, for the one God of the Old Testament is universally described as a personal being. Theologians often struggle with this, for the notion of a nonmaterial substance is very peculiar.

The classical model also raises difficulties about whether the One God of the Old Testament is the Father or the entire Trinity. The correct answer is the latter, but that leaves us with God behaving as a single person in the Old Testament and as three persons in the New.

The only other way out of the dilemma is to admit that there is no adequate analogy for God's nature, so we are faced with a mystery. In the last analysis this is necessarily true; yet God *has* revealed himself, and it is the task of theology to go as far as possible in making clear who he is and what he is like.

These acute difficulties with the classical model led the great Augustine to propose alternative models. His hope was to produce an analogy that would do greater justice to the two basic truths. As mentioned earlier, he was convinced that the best analogy was to be found in the human personality.

Augustine's idea, like most of his thought, has much to commend it. It grounds God's unity not in an impersonal substance but in personhood. It also eliminates the need for an ethereal substance. This model demands something in the human personality that corresponds to the three persons of the Trinity. The personality-role description provides exactly what is required.

First, the equality of the persons in the Godhead corresponds to the equality of the normal person's personality roles.

Second, just as the essential feature of normalcy in humans is the unity of the personality roles around a single will, so the Son and the Spirit accept the Father's will. Jesus' submission to the Father's will in Gethsemane shows this in practice, as does his response to Satan's temptation in the desert. In both cases Jesus was invited to violate the Father's will. These were attempts to split the Godhead. If the unthinkable had happened and Jesus had succumbed, the persons of the Godhead would be opposed to each other. Satan's temptations were a blasphemous attempt to make God dysfunctional. The attempt failed, of course, and the three persons of God—Father, Son and Spirit—retained their perfect unity and harmony.

Third, if we can think of the Trinity in this way, we illustrate a truth that has already been stated: having personality roles is healthy, not dysfunctional. Dysfunction arises when the roles fragment the will and make war on each other.

In this sinful world the personality roles in human beings never achieve the complete unity that only God exhibits, but we can approach it. When we do, we have mental health and we are ready for growth in holiness, learning to become like God in another way.

6

RESOLVING YOUR INNER TENSIONS

• • • • • • •

If you are *relatively "together" at the moment, you are* probably not conscious of your other personality roles; when you play a particular role, you *are* that person. So don't expect to become easily conscious of your other personality roles—especially if you have suppressed and rejected them as "not me."

Mapping out your roles takes effort, but it is well worth it. It is the first step toward bringing unity to your inner selves and thus overcoming inner compulsions.

Mapping Your Roles

As you examine your life, you will find that each relationship calls for a different kind of behavior. If you are a parent, you use a particular set of personality characteristics in your role as father or mother. If you are married, you relate differently to your spouse from the way you relate to your children. You may, for example, be authoritative as a parent but submissive as a spouse—or you may be easygoing with your children and defensive with your spouse.

How do you relate to your own parents? Usually our style as a son or daughter is different again. Write down your usual style in each of your family relationships, using table 2 as an example to guide you.

Father style	Dominating, committed, nurturing, protective
Son style	Submissive, respectful, supportive
Husband style	Masculine, manipulative, defensive

Table 2. An example of an individual's family role analysis

Next look at the way you relate at work. Do you pride yourself on your professionalism? Are you submissive to your boss? Try to characterize your style in each major relationship (boss, peers and subordinates).

Now think about your friendships. Try to define your style of relating with your friends too.

In each of these situations you operate in a role. The point of this exercise is to analyze how you uniquely fill those roles. Styles may be active or passive, open or withdrawn, protective, controlling, relaxed, defensive, fearful, confident, authoritative, rule-oriented, caring, people-pleasing and so on. If you find that several of these terms help describe how you act in one of your roles, write them all down.

Keep in mind too that you may need to describe some of your roles twice (or more) if you have more than one version of them.

For example, you may be one kind of son with your father and another kind of son with your mother. Be as specific and accurate about your roles as possible.

As you do this, you'll probably find that being honest about your undesirable traits is hard. Most of us tend to reject our bad sides as "not us." When our bad sides emerge, we tend to make excuses to distance ourselves from them: "I'm sorry I got angry at you this afternoon. I wasn't myself all day." In this exercise it's important to be as honest as possible; write down *all* the ways you relate to people, even if you think certain kinds of behavior aren't indicative of the "real" you. Perhaps you have an angry self with a bad temper, or a lustful self who objectifies members of the opposite sex. Table 3 provides an example of a more complete personality-role analysis that might result from this kind of brainstorming.

Mother style	Dominating, authoritarian, committed, defensive
Daughter style	Submissive, manipulative, respectful
Wife style	Feminine, manipulative
Boss style	Cool, professional, demanding, fair
Peer style	Competitive, self-possessed
Subordinate style	Respectful of status, crisp and organized
Friend style	Relaxed, confident, talkative

Table 3. Personality-role analysis involving family relationships, work relationships and friendships

Now try to group roles in which you show similar characteristics. Does your role with your children feel similar to your role with your subordinates at work? Is your relationship with your father or your mother similar to your relationship with your boss? You will probably be able to recognize a few distinctive styles of behavior that you slip into in different contexts. On your table, connect up these clusters of characteristics with lines.

At this point your aim is to identify a set of three or four similar roles that you play in different circumstances. Some of these are very much "you," and you feel pleased with them. Others you dislike but have to admit that you play them. Now, using these new role clusters, make your personality-role map. Table 4 provides an example.

Controller	Authoritarian, comes out at home, likes ordered environment, disciplinarian
Professional	Cool, effective, controlled, organized
Confider	Talkative, uses poor judgment, tends to gossip, loyal
Belle	Feminine manipulator, gives to men based on expectation of strong masculine protection in return, people-pleaser

Table 4. One possible personality-role map drawn from table 3

At this stage take a break from your brainstorming and then come back to it. Have you been totally honest with yourself about your unappealing traits? As you go back over your tables, pray for the strength and discernment to be honest. When you are satisfied with your personality-role map, it's time to look more closely at the origins of your roles.

How Parents Help Shape Personality

Because personality roles are created in the context of relationships, it should be no surprise that they first emerge as we relate to our parents. As I have discussed earlier, the all-powerful figure of Mother has the ability to mold her child's responses in many ways. She lavishes approval, support, comfort and caresses on the baby who performs as expected. When the baby says "Mama" for the first time, for example, the behavior is rewarded with massive approval. Mother will signal with equal clarity when Baby has displeased her. This reward-and-punishment system molds children during their most formative years. Essentially the child is being directed how to behave in a role within a relationship; the baby is learning his or her first personality role.

As Father comes more into the picture, the child learns how to respond appropriately and gain the rewards of approval from this new source. Since the father is a different person, a different response is required. What works with Mother may not work with Father, so new actions are tested out. Bit by bit the infant learns how to win the responses he seeks—usually forms of approval, but not always. (Acting fussy, for example, probably won't help Baby gain approval, but it may help him get his diaper changed faster.) In any event, the child is learning how to play expected roles.

So far I have been talking as if each relationship produces a single personality role. Life, of course, is not that simple. Because mothers and fathers themselves have developed conflicting personality roles, they are not always consistent in their childrearing.

One day a mother may resent her baby's demands on her and be severe and angry, cowing the child into submission. Later, feeling guilty, she may swing to the opposite extreme and lavish attention on the confused child. Babies are remarkable learners, however, and soon the child develops two patterns of behavior to match the mother's two styles. The angry, dominating style produces a nervous, submissive child. The overgenerous mother, on the other hand, produces a resentful child who knows that rebellious behavior is effective in controlling the guilt-ridden mother. The mother-child relationship splits into two relationships between two pairs of roles.

As the child grows, he learns by imitation as well as by reaction. A young boy soon learns from an angry father to be rude and insulting to his mother, or from a gentle father to be kind to her. How often we see children imitating their parents' mannerisms and turns of phrase. For better or worse, we copy our parents.

The process of imitation may also cause dissociation into mutually opposing roles. In seeking Dad's approval a little girl may first copy Mother's feminine ways and then learn that her father really wanted a little boy. So she also learns to be a tomboy but never stops imitating her mother's feminine characteristics. The two roles produced by this process obviously dislike one another.

Let's take another situation where parental dynamics can cause dissociation into mutually opposing roles. A father looks to his daughter to give him the feminine responses his wife denies him. This makes Mother jealous, and she punishes the child by emotionally withdrawing when her daughter and her husband are interacting. Because the girl doesn't want to lose her mother's love, the girl learns to deceive her; she becomes Daddy's girl in secret with him and demurely distances herself when Mother is present. The possibilities are endless, but the rule is clear: mixed signals produce conflicting behavior and opposing roles.

Now it's time to explore your own childhood. First consider whether you had a double-role relationship with either parent. This is likely if your mother or father was angry or alcoholic or had any other problem that caused very uneven styles of training and modeling (such as the emotional upheaval that accompanies the loss of a spouse through death or divorce). Now write down the roles you played for your mother and father. Where there are two, write them both down.

Second, compare the roles you played for your mother and father. Were they in tension?

Third, compare the personality-role map you drew up earlier with these early personality roles from your childhood. Can you see how the child's roles developed into your adult pattern of roles?

Finally, consider how you may have imitated one or both of your parents. Are you still doing it? Which of your current relationships is like the ones you had (and perhaps still have) with your father and mother? Note your results on your map. Your changing map might look something like tables 5 and 6.

Relationship	Style
With father	Very submissive; attempt to placate his anger
With mother	Compete for father's attention; manipulative
With husband	Passive and submissive; fear arousing his anger
With best friend	Tend to dominate and compete
With teenage son	Controlling; fearful of his growing masculinity
With teenage daughter	Dominating and demanding
With boss	Very submissive

Table 5. Relationship styles with others

Relationship	Like Style with Mother	Like Style with Father
With husband		x
With best friend	x	
With teenage son		x
With teenage daughter	x	
With boss		x

Table 6. How parental relationships are copied in later relationships

In the above example, a woman who learned a passive and compliant style of relating to her father finds herself falling into that pattern with authority figures—especially males. Similarly, the role she learned from her mother comes to the fore in relationships with females perceived as peers.

Understanding Your Compulsions

Now that you understand your roles and their origins better, you can use this information to begin to understand troublesome compulsive behavior—why you find yourself doing the things you don't want to do.

As I discussed earlier, our compulsions are markers that signal the presence of a suppressed role. Because our inner selves fiercely resist imprisonment, we release the pressure they exert on us by placating them with a self-indulgence. Thus we maintain equilibrium through our compulsive behavior—stuffing ourselves with sweets, taking drugs, looking at pornography, or worse. As we have seen, Paul expresses this inner struggle clearly in Romans 7. When he cries, "Who will rescue me from this body of death?" he speaks for every Christian who ever lived.

We Christians often regard the suppressed personality role and the compulsive behavior associated with it as "the flesh." Although we try to put it to death, we quickly find it impossible to destroy part of ourselves.

The first step toward eliminating compulsive behavior, then, is to stop treating it simplistically. Simply trying harder to eliminate it doesn't work, because what we are really trying to do is eliminate part of ourselves.

The second step is to make sure we have honestly identified the compulsion in all of its ugliness. It may be drugs or alcohol. It may be overeating or undereating. It may be anger or passive withdrawal. It may be sexual promiscuity with total strangers, or it may be frigidity with a beloved spouse. It may be orderly and easy to hide or disorderly and hard to hide. There are many kinds of compulsions.

What are your compulsive patterns? Observe yourself by recording a diary. Pay careful attention to the events that precede a self-indulgent session. Over a period a pattern will usually emerge. A triggering event will repeat itself, followed each time with the despised self-indulgence.

Having identified your compulsions, look again at your personality-role map. How do you feel when you indulge in each compulsive behavior? Is this feeling associated in your mind with a particular role? If the personality role is not too deeply suppressed, you will soon recognize it as the source of the compulsive behavior. To identify a deeply suppressed personality role, however, you may need the help of a therapist.

Now try to identify the controlling roles that suppress the angry or frustrated role. Why do they hate or fear it?

Often it is easy to see the answer. Warring roles tend to be polarized into opposites; that is what *dissociation* means. The intellect, for example, may become associated with one personality role, while the emotions become linked with another. Naturally these roles don't understand one another, which often leads to mutual dislike: forceful, angry roles are at odds with compliant, people-pleasing roles; sensual roles conflict with legalistic, controlling roles; spontaneous, emotional roles oppose and are opposed by more orderly, controlled roles; and so on.

Shame is the language that a dominant role uses to express its dislike of a suppressed role who defeats it from time to time by demanding to be satisfied with a compulsive behavior. The behavior feels shameful because the dominant role can't help but give in to it; knowledge of the suppressed role itself feels shameful because it is part of the self. Shame reflects the pain of having personality roles that dislike each other.

What are you ashamed of? Which role lets you down by its behavior? Which part of you dislikes the behavior and feels the shame? When you have answered these questions, you have identified a source of personality-role tension.

Take another look at your personality-role map, and try to pinpoint mutual fear and dislike between your parts. Those fears and hatreds are the problems we must solve to achieve wholeness. Our personality roles must learn to cooperate smoothly and respectfully, each taking its place as needed.

The Risk of Change

Alan's compulsion was masturbation. On the outside he was very intellectual. He was also a serious and thoughtful Christian, so his defeats were a great embarrassment to him.

After much soul-searching, Alan was able to trace his compulsion to masturbate to a suppressed inner self—an emotional self that had never been affirmed. Alan's father was a cold, remote man who gave his son approval only if he sought it. Even as an adult, Alan still initiated every contact between them, for he had a soft, loving side that needed his father's love. This perpetual rejection of Alan's loving, emotional role caused him to bury it; he not only feared being hurt further but also feared experiencing his own anger at being rejected.

Although Alan put his unemotional, intellectual role in charge, the emotional Alan demanded release from time to time. He was not allowed out in the presence of others, of course; unleashing all that emotional energy in public would be too dangerous. Instead Alan allowed him out in private, by masturbating.

Once he identified the suppressed inner self responsible for his compulsive behavior, Alan was able to begin the process of integrating that role with his other roles in a healthy way and thus conquer his compulsion. Once you discover the role responsible for your compulsive behavior, you too can move forward.

But be warned: even when you do begin to achieve integration of your rejected self and freedom from a particular kind of compulsive behavior, your life will not always get easier. When you start to probe deeply in this way, you can disturb the equilibrium that giving in to compulsive behavior has allowed you. If your inner tensions are very strong, releasing and trying to integrate a hated personality role may seriously disrupt your life.

Take Jane. You met her in chapter three; she was the compliant, submissive wife who depended on her husband, Joe, completely. You also met a second Jane, a "forceful Jane" who contained the strength that the outer Jane was missing. I have already described how I made contact with this forceful inner self and how in time she (like her dominant counterpart, "gentle Jane") came under the rule of Jesus. Now she was still forceful but trustworthy as well; in difficult situations she competently took over to relieve gentle Jane. Jane's displays of strength were becoming more and more constructive.

Earlier I described how Jane's supportive husband, Joe, appreciated the positive changes in her life. To be honest, I didn't tell the whole story. He didn't always like the new side of his wife that was emerging. She was sometimes argumentative now; often she would express herself forcefully. Perhaps even more disturbing to him, the dependent, clinging, gentle Jane no longer needed him to protect her from life. Whereas before she could not even face workmen who came to their home, she could now deal with more demanding situations by switching to her "forceful Jane" role. Not only the old equilibrium in Jane's life was breaking down, but the equilibrium in their marriage as well. Joe, finding himself with a more aggressive wife who didn't make him feel as needed, often longed for the old passive Jane. Their marriage felt the strain.

Jane and Joe were discovering that change is dangerous territory. Wholeness does come, but painfully and slowly. When our equilibrium is disturbed, things may actually seem to get worse, tempting us to turn back from our journey of self-discovery. That's one reason it may be necessary to seek the help and support of a therapist when you are attempting to resolve severe inner tensions. He or she can help keep you on track when your resolve to overcome compulsive behavior crumbles.

Talking to Ourselves
Before you can resolve the inner tensions between roles, they must begin to understand one another. As in any relationship, this involves communication.

We all talk to ourselves. Once we grasp that our personality is a cluster of roles, this should not surprise us. Personality roles usually do talk to one another; that is what self-talk is. Suppressed roles cause problems for us precisely because they have been left out of this conversation.

Talking to your excluded personality roles is important. This will probably seem a strange idea at first; most of us do not easily admit to holding conversations with ourselves at all, much less with rejected inner selves! It will also seem hard to do. It is painful to admit that the parts that shame me actually are part of me. And because suppressed personality roles are not used to being included in our inner conversations, they can be difficult to talk to and even harder to hear. If you seek wholeness, however, engaging suppressed selves in conversation is exactly what you must do.

For a well-adjusted person, the exercises of this chapter will have been interesting, but not earth-shaking or even difficult. If your efforts have distressed you, though, you will need the help of a good therapist to clarify the parts of yourself and the tensions between them. If you are in any doubt at all, by all means get help. In chapter eight I will point out the danger of self-therapy under such circumstances.

With the support of a therapist, you must take an interior journey in search of your suppressed inner self. Your personality-role map may have already revealed who you are seeking. It is now time to meet your problem personality roles face to face.

7

STARTING THE INNER JOURNEY

• • • • • • •

Most of us *don't suppress our disliked personality* roles very deeply. If this is true of you, your personality-role map will probably have revealed your internal "problem people." Those of us with more deeply suppressed roles may need the help of a counselor to identify them; in any case, the personality-role map you have drawn can serve as a starting point for discussion.

Once we have identified a suppressed personality role, how do we begin actually releasing and integrating it?

The very first step we must take is to acknowledge that the journey within is frightening. We fear confronting the parts of ourselves that we have imprisoned. That fear is understandable. Rather than allowing our fear to hinder us, however, we should embrace it as a reminder that we do not have the power to undertake this journey alone. God must go before us. Thus we pray as we make this journey, asking our heavenly Father, who knows us intimately, for help and protection. We purify ourselves by confessing sin and seeking the Father's forgiveness. And we allow ourselves to experience once more his acceptance. Finally, we call upon the Holy Spirit, who dwells within every Christian, to lead us into truth.

Once I had identified my suppressed roles by making a personality-role map and had prayed over the inner journey I was about to take toward them, I gave these suppressed inner selves names. Because giving a suppressed personality role a name helps to identify it more clearly, I advise the people I counsel to do the same. Usually they use a nickname or some variant of their own name. Some people choose a pet name given to them by a parent. Others purposely choose an ugly name. Often these names are very revealing. One woman's degree of shame about her sexuality surfaced when she decided to call her inner sexual self Sleaze.

Once you name your suppressed inner self, try to speak to it. Aim to understand and listen to its voice. If that personality role "comes out" on specific occasions, talk to yourself about how he or she feels when in control. In other words, try to grasp how it feels to *be* that personality role. As you gain empathy for this rejected part of yourself, it will be easier to draw it into your inner conversation, which is a necessary step toward total self-acceptance and wholeness.

Finding Your Missing Pieces
Now try to explore your inner world by visualizing it. With eyes closed, try to imagine the people you have imprisoned inside. If you are not inclined toward introspection, this may take a lot of effort, concentration and time. You may feel strong resistance to the whole process. After all, you suppressed these parts of yourself for good reason.

If you can press on, let your imagination roam freely to seek the part of yourself that is imprisoned. Explore the dark spaces in your mind. Listen for crying voices coming from where the hidden pain is felt. My friends have found their inner people in strange and fearful places. Some were found in settings where they suffered long ago, such as dark rooms or closets. Many of these inner people were children. They had been split off to absorb the pain, shame and rage that the child couldn't handle.

You may find it helpful to visualize a closed door. Go up to it and listen carefully. Can you hear someone crying behind it? Try to ignore the fear that urges you to run away; instead, call out reassurances to the person on the other side. Tell him or her that you are there to help and comfort, not to condemn or punish. Persist in the face of rejection. Try to make friends, but do not yet attempt to explore the reasons for their pain or anger. On this first journey it is enough to make contact. Then say goodby and promise to return.

Building the Inner Relationship

You will need to return to this crying voice many times. As you come closer to making contact with the hurting person behind it, you will probably be shocked at the intensity of emotion you experience. Don't be afraid. This person has been buried inside you all along, and you have survived till now.

Try to see these lonely, frightened or angry inner selves as needy. The frightened, hurt ones need you to open their prison doors and hold them. If you see them as weeping children, put your arms around them; they probably carry the pain of rejection experienced early in life. Children tend to blame themselves for everything that happens to them. When something bad happens to them, part of them splits off to bear the shame. This dissociated part believes, then, that it is bad; and that feeling is intensified as the outer self continually rejects it. (After all, if I am rejected by myself, I *must* be bad.) This is the time to reverse the flow of rejection. Offer acceptance to this hurt inner self and bring it home.

Above all, make it clear to this inner person that you and God love and accept them and want to know about the source of their hurt. In this way you extend the peace of God to new parts of your personality, as I helped "forceful Jane" to do. Many people find it helpful to go through this process with a counselor who is a Christian. In the end, however, the task of self-acceptance is yours alone.

If your rejected role is angry, expect to be repulsed many times. Try to understand the anger. It may be important to validate it. In my experience, child abuse always leads to anger, and rightly so. To abuse a child is a violation of justice that angers God too. Jesus minced no words on the subject: "It would be better . . . to be thrown into the sea with a millstone tied around [your] neck than . . . to cause one of these little ones to sin" (Luke 17:2).[1]

Listen to the rage of the inner child who experienced abuse. Validate her anger and sense of injustice. Say, "You have a right to be angry. What was done to you was wrong." If you accept her anger, a child who had no protector may now find a protector in you. An authority figure, such as a pastoral counselor or therapist, may help you do this. As a pastor, I find that I can help others validate their anger at the injustices they suffered. I let them know that it's more than just okay to feel the anger—it's appropriate. And I share in the feeling of anger with them.

When the anger has been heard, ask yourself: "Do I want to go on being angry?" You have a right to, but do you *want* to? As a Christian, your ultimate aim should be to move beyond legal rights to grace. If you have trouble letting go of your anger, let yourself experience it awhile longer. If you continue to have trouble letting go of your anger, consider the damage being done by it as it turns to bitterness. Do you really want to allow the damage originally inflicted on you by others to go on? Usually you can bring the angry role to renounce the desire to go on being angry. This may begin a process of dealing with parents or others who did the damage. Sometimes this even leads to confession and the restoration of a bad relationship, transforming it to a new one based on respect.

More often, however, those who abused us are unable or unwilling to pursue reconciliation. If so, we must seek to let go of any desire for vengeance and judgment. That is as far as forgiveness can go in such cases. This difficult issue of forgiveness will be explored more fully in chapter eleven. For now, your aim is to release your rejected personality role's anger so that it can be brought into inner fellowship with your other personality roles.

Working in Harmony with Myself

The next stage in self-acceptance is to establish mutual respect among your roles.

Julie had suppressed her femininity very thoroughly. Her every gesture was firm and masculine. Her clothes were severely tailored and drab-colored. Over time she gradually made contact with her feminine side and acknowledged her fear of its sexuality, which until this time had been allowed to emerge only in sporadic bouts of sexual promiscuity.

As she accepted and began talking to her feminine side, she wanted to learn how to let it "out" in a healthy way. (She called this side of herself June, her birthday month.) Because Julie was still a little fearful of letting June loose, she planned a safe excursion in which the chance of meeting a man would be minimal. Julie went shopping for a new wardrobe; but this time the selection would be June's responsibility.

The result was amazing. The next time Julie came to see me, she was wearing a soft, flowing dress in a striking shade of pink. She had a new hairstyle and was reveling in her freedom to be a woman. Her feminine side felt accepted and affirmed. She was now a whole woman who no longer tried to suppress her femininity.

Like Julie, we must bring all the fragments of our personality into cooperation. Each has a distinct role to play; all are needed if we are to be whole. If the rejected role is angry or has immoral tendencies, letting it out feels very dangerous—especially for us Christians. Because the Bible exhorts us to "die to self," we believe that we should try to kill our troublesome, suppressed inner selves. As we have seen, however, this is not possible. Because our inner selves are part of us, they can't be killed—only avoided and suppressed or confronted and integrated. Paradoxically, it is not until our inner selves are accepted and integrated into the total self that we can actually begin the process of "dying to self"; only then can we stop being self-consumed, alternately trying to placate and hide our rejected inner selves.

This is not to say that we shouldn't proceed with caution when we let our rejected roles surface. Like Julie, we may need to move slowly, avoiding situations where we are tempted to sin. This is different, however, from continuing to reject the role as "not me."

I call the process of accepting and integrating a problem role *rehabilitation*. Rehabilitation begins with self-appreciation. Julie, for example, had to accept that her feminine role is not evil. Because June had often taken over and led her into sexual promiscuity, this was difficult. As they began to talk to each other, however, Julie began to see that there was more to June than illicit sex. June also contained her emotional, tender, sensitive side; she was keyed in not only to sexual pleasure but also to the aesthetic pleasures of color, shape and music. Julie badly needed these missing parts of herself.

Every suppressed personality role contains some part of yourself. As long as it is rejected, you remain incomplete. Realizing that you need what this "ugly" role has—that it, in fact, contains some of your gifts—can change your view of it, making you open to accept it.

Once this appreciation process has been started, your inner conversation can change rapidly. Instead of ostracizing and vilifying the suppressed role, your dominant role can begin discussing with it how to cooperate in efforts to pursue godly behavior.

Sometimes an ugly personality role blossoms under the sunshine of self-acceptance in just a few weeks.

Acceptance soon progresses to trust. Bit by bit the rejected role has to be allowed its place. The repertoire of roles is then complete. They all wait just beneath the surface of the personality, each ready to step forward and take control when needed. In a moment of tenderness, the tender role slips into action. Under challenge, a stronger, fiercer part takes over. Like Jesus, the person moves easily and naturally from gentleness to fierceness, from cuddling children to angrily confronting injustice. Emotional wholeness has come.

At this point the sharp distinction I have drawn between roles eases a little. We become less aware of them as separate parts of the self, and our self-talk comes more naturally. Though we are still aware of playing different roles, we are at peace with ourselves.

8
SEEKING
HELP

. . . .

I once read *about a crazy man who performed* surgery on his own body. Using a local anesthetic, he cut into his own flesh and carried out an appendectomy.

Surgery of the soul has its own special difficulties. Usually it cannot be self-performed, because the delusions that make treatment necessary also make treatment difficult. In any case, most of those who try to do "soul surgery" alone soon find that they need the support of a therapist or pastoral counselor more than they thought. The road to self-discovery can take unexpected and unnerving turns. Painful memories of abuse may surface, for example, causing a crisis that one is ill-equipped to handle.

My intention in this book is to help those who simply want to gain self-understanding, not to provide a do-it-yourself guide for those who should be getting the help of a therapist or pastoral counselor. As you explore your own self-roles, don't push yourself to expose any that are deeply suppressed on your own. Your suppressed personality roles may carry with them hidden memories that you are not ready to face.

When to Seek Help

How do you know if you need the help of a therapist or counselor?

This is not always an easy question to answer. Most of us do not suffer from anything as severe as full-blown multiple-personality disorder, which clearly must be treated by a mental-health professional. Nor do we feel we fit the definition of a completely healthy self, whose self-roles coexist without tension or mutual hostility. Most of us who struggle with compulsive behavior fall somewhere in between: the childhood trauma we experienced was significant, but not significant enough to cause total dissociation into entirely separate personalities.

When deciding whether to seek help, you need to decide where you think you fall on the spectrum of dissociation discussed in chapter two. As you may recall, this spectrum has distinct divisions that can help us locate ourselves. The most important of these is accessibility of memories. The greater the childhood trauma and resulting dissociation, the more likely it is that one suppressed self-role has taken responsibility for painful memories. This association with a hateful experience causes deep alienation between remembering and nonremembering selves. The dominant, remembering selves *want* to lose the memory for self-protection—and to do so they must continue to reject the self-role that retains access to it. As we have seen, compulsive behavior results from this suppression process.

Not everyone has hidden memories, of course, because not everyone has experienced severe childhood trauma. The signs that such potentially devastating memories *may* exist include the following:

☐ a substantial absence of memories from the early years of

childhood (from about four years old on)

☐ compulsive behavior that has no basis in the revealed self

☐ an inability to function in some normal way (for example, an inability to feel emotion)

If you experience any of these symptoms, do not try to pursue self-exploration and healing alone. As you get in touch with suppressed roles, you may well encounter repressed memories—and the intense pain they carry—for the first time. Although it is important to come to terms with repressed memories in order to bring personality roles into harmony, doing so under the guidance of a therapist will ensure that you don't become overwhelmed by more than you can handle.

Who Should Help: Therapist or Exorcist?

Perhaps you have decided that your compulsive behavior, memory loss or inability to function normally in some way indicates that you need help. But what kind of help do you need? Because those of us with severely dissociated personality roles feel as if inner forces compel us to act, we may wonder if we are victims of some kind of demonic activity. If you are wondering this, the following section is intended either to assure you that your problems are fundamentally emotional in nature or to encourage you to seek competent spiritual help.

In working with people who have deeply divided selves, I sometimes encounter some very wicked alter personalities, particularly in cases of ritual abuse. Such personalities are often suicidal or self-mutilating; sometimes they declare their love for evil and their hatred of God. This kind of evil is palpable and chilling. How does one decide if these are merely dark alter personalities or demonic entities?

Although the Bible leaves no doubt about the reality of demonic entities in the spirit world, Western Christians have been hesitant to acknowledge them—largely out of fear of looking ridiculous in our materialistic, rationalistic culture. Our culture's extreme skepticism about the existence of supernatural forces such as demons has begun to fade, however, making open discussion about demonic activity possible. Scott Peck has been at the forefront of this discussion. In his book *People of the Lie,* he tells of delivering people from demonic possession.

> Of course I did not believe that possession existed. In fifteen years of busy psychiatric practice I had never seen anything faintly resembling a case. . . . So I decided to go out and look. . . . The third case [I investigated] turned out to be the real thing.
>
> Since then I have also been deeply involved with another case of genuine possession. In both cases I was privileged to be present at their successful exorcisms. The vast majority of cases in the literature are those of possession by minor demons. These two were highly unusual in that both were cases of Satanic possession. I now know Satan is real. I have met it.[1]

If you feel like you're the victim of an alter personality who makes you do things you don't want to do, are you, like Peck's clients, under the influence of a demon? Not necessarily. C. S. Lewis warned us that the enemy has two strategies: to persuade us that he does not exist and to encourage us to become obsessed with him. In our current cultural climate we are becoming more inclined to be obsessive about him. This leads to "spiritualizing" problems that are fundamentally emotional.

Such spiritualizing is dangerous. When pastors or Christian counselors falsely diagnose an alter personality as demonic, they put the people in their care on an emotional roller coaster. Because a part of someone's personality can't be cast out, the prospect of an exorcism raises false hope. Many Christians are only too willing to cling to exorcism as a way out. Being exorcised, after all, does not require the hard work of facing and integrating alienated roles. This is why some people struggling with compulsive, sinful behavior hastily conclude that they have a demon of lust or greed. It is easier to blame a demon than admit that a part of one's own personality is responsible for undesirable behavior. As Romans 7 indicates, owning up to compulsive inner selves is precisely what caused Paul great psychic pain.

When you are trying to discern whether you or someone else is demon-possessed, it is important to remember that the Bible nowhere ascribes sinful behavior to the presence of unclean spirits. Instead, demons seem to cause sickness and bizarre behavior. Satan certainly does attack us with temptations; but feeling and giving in to what feels like an overwhelming temptation does not result from demon *possession*. It results from demonic attack, which is not the same thing. Another reason for our propensity to confuse demonic attack and demonic possession lies in our misunderstanding of King James English. The King James Bible often translates the Greek verb *to have* as "to be possessed of." In Elizabethan English this is correct, for to say "I am possessed of a ring" means simply that I have it in my possession. In modern English, however, we take "I am possessed of" to mean that something possesses *me*—that is, owns me and exerts control over me. Thus we read the King James Bible's "he is possessed of a demon" to mean "he is under the total control of a demon."

The Bible never says that anyone is "demon-possessed"; it simply notes that the person "has a demon" or is "demonized." The term *unclean spirit* helps us picture what's really going on. A demonic entity lurking inside a person contaminates rather than controls. It is a dirty "thing," quite distinct from the alter personalities, hiding in the inner confusion of the deeply divided personality.

So when should the presence of a demonic entity be suspected?

Bizarre, evil and unusually persistent compulsions that a competent counselor cannot explain in terms of suppressed personality roles often indicate the presence of a demon. Unlike hostile personality roles, unclean spirits typically have no interest in human contact, nor do they interact in a human way. When they speak, they often spout forth an inhumanly matter-of-fact hatred for life. They seem dead and soulless inside. One cannot *know* them.

Demons are most commonly found in victims of satanic ritual abuse. It is, after all, the aim of ritual abusers to gain demonic power over a vulnerable child, so that part of him feels compelled to keep putting himself at the cult's disposal. A child whose personality has dissociated several times loses his fragile sense of self-boundaries, and a demonic entity is easily hidden in the confusion.

What strategy should pastors use to deliver such people from demons? Unfortunately, neglect of what the Bible and experienced Christian ministers can teach us about demons has left most of ill-equipped to confront them. Hence we are vulnerable to being deceived by such spirits when we do meet them. The unclean spirit typically tries to hide behind alter personalities (or, in a less dissociated person, behind personality roles) so that the pastor believes it doesn't really exist.

Thus once an unclean spirit has been located, a pastor should *not* attempt to find out its name; instead, he or she should only try to identify its characteristics. The idea that knowing the demon's name gives one power over it comes from magic rituals, not from Christianity; such a belief is found in ancient papyrus incantation scripts and medieval occult writing such as the Cabala rather than the Bible. (Even in the case of Legion, the one biblical account of demonization where a spirit name is mentioned, Jesus commands the spirits to depart before asking their name; evidently he did not need the name to exorcise them.)

Those who bear the name of Jesus can simply command the unclean spirit to leave, referring to it by its character—"spirit of death," "spirit of mutilation" or whatever. Using our authority in the name of Jesus this way, combined with persistent prayer, is sufficient to deliver anyone who is truly demonized. When deliverance occurs, deeply divided people who had come to an impasse in bringing their personality roles to support one another find themselves able to move ahead.

We in the West are children in these matters, but we are learning. As we grow in understanding, we discover anew the awesome power of the name of Jesus. That is our greatest weapon in this fight and our major contribution to the field of psychology.

What to Expect in Counseling

Though demonization is real, the majority of us suffering from compulsive behavior need a psychotherapist rather than an exorcist. What can you expect from a counseling session with a competent psychotherapist or pastoral counselor? What does it look like when someone helps you identify and integrate suppressed roles that may carry repressed memories?

As you might expect, there is no one formulaic sequence of events that every person must experience to find wholeness. There are, however, some events that do occur during many counseling sessions with people suffering from dissociated personality roles.

When a member of my congregation comes to me for help with compulsive behavior, we explore together the different parts of his personality. Usually this involves studying relationships with parents. We then try to bring each self-role into submission to Jesus, so that it can contribute to the whole person's spiritual growth.

If the compulsive behavior continues at this stage, my parishioner, his or her therapist and I may conclude that a part of the self is missing. If so, we then explore memories. When a person remembers little or nothing from a significant chunk of his or her childhood, we conclude that the person is suppressing a personality role that carries painful memories.

At that point we pray together. In pastoral care of the soul we are highly dependent on God's help. It is his wisdom we seek and his truth that must be exposed. Whatever the hidden depths that may be revealed, we affirm together God's power to deal with it. If there is guilt, he brings forgiveness. If there is shame, he brings love. If there is rejection, he brings acceptance. We build faith together in God's trustworthiness and his ability to bring good from evil.

Then I encourage the person to relax, close their eyes, put their hand in God's and begin an inner journey to search for their hidden inner self. Although the person knows, of course, that I believe they have suppressed a part of the self, they have no idea of what exactly I am expecting to find. I simply ask open-ended questions, scrupulously avoiding suggestion. Such a conversation may go something like this:

"Is it dark or light?"

"It's completely dark."

"Can you hear anything?"

"No."

"Can you see anything?"

"No."

"What are you standing on?"

"Some kind of stone or concrete."

"Smooth or rough?"

"Rough."

"Is it flat?"

"No, it slopes down."

"Can you walk down it?"

"Yes. It's getting a little lighter. I can feel a wall alongside me. Now I'm in a passage. Now I'm going down some stairs."

"Keep going; keep all your senses alert."

"It's getting colder. I'm feeling frightened."

"Don't be afraid. God is walking with you. Nothing can harm you. Trust him."

"I can hear crying."

"Go toward the sound."

"I have found a door. It's locked. The crying is coming from behind it. I can feel waves of fear now."

We pause for a prayer, asking God to protect and to intercede for the weeping person.

"Can you open the door?"

"Yes."

"What can you see?"

"It's my bedroom. I can see a girl crying on the bed. She is me."

"Can you comfort her?"

"Yes, I have my arms around her. She's clinging to me."

"How are you feeling?"

"Very calm and relaxed. She feels the same."

"Will she speak to me?"

"Yes."

Then a conversation with this inner person may follow. Sometimes her responses are relayed through the outer personality; other times the inner person speaks directly to me in a changed voice or a different style. I try to befriend this new person. This is easy if they want support and encouragement; if they are angry, however, they may verbally attack me. Refusing to return anger for anger, I persistently express understanding and liking. Eventually the inner person comes to trust me. At that point I ask if I can help in any way. Although the answer is usually no at this stage, we have established friendly contact. I say goodby and request to meet with them again.

The person I'm counseling then closes the door and journeys back up the stairs and passageway until she opens her eyes. We thank God for his help and then talk quietly together. We explore the other self's age, appearance and feelings. Usually the person expresses antagonism or fear toward the suppressed personality role. I reassure them that my speaking with that inner person does not mean that he or she will "take over" their personality.

Each time we meet the process becomes easier. Soon the person may be making contact with this part of the self quite frequently. We are all becoming friends. Now that trust has deepened, I can start to ask the inner person for information. "Why are you so sad? Why are you angry? Can I help?"

When an inner self is angry, I often find him to be a victim of injustice who feels powerless. If so, he usually begins to share painful memories with me—memories of abandonment, rejection, coldness, harshness and other forms of physical, verbal and sexual abuse. As he does, I try to be affirming. "It was not your fault," I say. "No one could blame you. You are *not* bad." To validate the inner self's anger, I (acting in my role as an authority figure) may show my own anger at the abuse he suffered; I may even declare God's anger at these injustices. After anger has been experienced, I invite the inner self to let go of the anger, lest holding on to it do further damage to him.

I then encourage the dominant self-role and suppressed self-role to work together. I try to break down mutual hostility by challenging the person's idea that the inner self is bad. I point out the inner self's good points and how useful they would be if he were allowed to play his role; I help him understand that to keep his other self locked away is to perpetuate the cycle that his abusers began. In time, acceptance comes.

The most important moment of this whole process is when the new self-role is drawn into the person's already existent relationship with Jesus. To see an alienated inner self yield to the lordship of Christ is almost as exhilarating as leading someone to faith in the first place.

Now the person is well on the way to wholeness. We plan encounters in which the new self-role can safely emerge and play his part. With a little practice this becomes routine; the person is able to slip into each self-role as circumstances demand. He has become emotionally whole.

Hidden Memories: The Current Controversy

Those who emerge from a process such as I've just described need the support of a counselor for more than one reason. As we've discussed, people often need an experienced guide to help them explore their inner terrain because they have been conditioned to deny the existence of suppressed inner selves. Furthermore, even if a person does manage to connect with an inner self on her own, the painful memories that the inner self carries may cause her further trauma if she lacks a counselor's emotional support.

To these let me add another important reason that people seeking to recover inner selves and hidden memories may need the emotional support of a counselor or therapist. Sometimes no one else believes them. Family members who perpetrated the abuse often deny their involvement, and other members, unwilling to face ugly family dynamics, may choose not to believe the victim. Given the media's recent close coverage of cases where people have admitted to making false accusations out of malice or confusion, even people outside a victim's family system may be hesitant to offer support.

People who recall torture and sexual abuse inflicted on them during a satanic sect's rituals stand an even slimmer chance of being believed. To believe them, one must accept the existence of a widespread satanic network with connections powerful enough to make evidence routinely disappear.[2]

This crisis—over to what extent those who "recover" hidden memories of abuse can and should be believed—continues to grow, in part because memories come to people as adults, many years after the purported abuse. Therapists exploring their clients' hidden memories are finding sexual and ritual abuse all over the place; yet police following up such stories do not always find corroborating evidence. Is the current focus on "hidden memories" a psychological breakthrough or a sensational fad?

This crisis has actually been brewing for decades. It began back when Freud was first pioneering the exploration of the inner mind and discovered that his female patients were haunted by apparent memories of incest. At first Freud took these memories at face value. Because he held a distinguished place in Viennese society and knew many of the fathers whose integrity was in question, however, he eventually succumbed to pressure to find another explanation for these memories. Eventually he came to theorize that these "memories" of incest were actually fantasies.

Freud theorized that his patients led a tempestuous inner sex life, free from the normal restraints governing external conduct. In this way he came to propose the existence of the id, that bundle of uncontrolled passions dwelling in every heart. What scandalized society at the time soon became orthodox doctrine in psychology. Psychoanalysts aimed to explore this dark inner life of suppressed passion and to free their patients from its tensions.

Disappointment with the results over the years has caused the influence of Freud's psychoanalytic model to wane; his basic assumption that early memories are often fantasies is today widely rejected. People in therapy who come to remember incest or other abuse are now taken at their word—not told that they are remembering imaginary events lurking in their subconscious mind. Most therapists today maintain that refusing to believe a victim further victimizes him or her. The client *must* be believed.

Like Freud, therapists and pastoral counselors face a choice. If they believe that memories of childhood are factual, then they must minister to a society in which incest and child abuse are much more common than anyone had previously suspected—a society where secretly hurting adults act out their pain by victimizing dependent and emotionally vulnerable children, making the family a place of horror. The only alternative route that therapists and counselors can take is Freud's. In other words, they can assume that such "memories" are actually dredged up from the dark corners of the child's soul. This approach implies that childhood innocence is a myth—that from infancy the child's mind is not only sexual but indeed violent. In this scenario, civilization's role is to impose order and morality on the dark chaos within.

People must be helped to see early memories as delusions.

The stakes in this choice are high. If counselors convince their clients that their memories are false when they are not, they deepen their emotional damage. Keep in mind that abuse victims are often told by their abusers that if they tell, no one will believe them—even worse, that they will be rejected and punished. Imagine the devastation when the all-powerful therapist—the very one to whom the client looked for help—now fulfills that prophecy.

On the other hand, what if the client is transferring to a father or uncle the false memories of childhood? Child abuse is a crime, punishable by imprisonment. Increasingly, recovered memories are being accepted as evidence in court. What if they are inaccurate? The therapist has participated in a process that may destroy an innocent family.

As more and more cases of child abuse have been uncovered while children are still small and able to remember, we have come to know how widespread child abuse really is. That's why many therapists and counselors today have made a general policy of believing clients. This does not mean, of course, that *all* memories of abuse are accurate. Mistakes can be made. Given that most people who claim to have been abused seem to be telling the truth, however, we as counselors have little choice but to believe alleged abuse victims, trusting careful investigation and judicial wisdom to catch up with people who make false claims. In my experience, therapists and pastors working as a team have the best chance of being able to distinguish authentic memories from those that are not.

Why Suffer Alone?

If your childhood traumas were mild, your self-roles are most likely accessible, carrying with them no suppressed memories. In that case, self-study of your personality roles will help you gain more control over your behavior as you seek to grow in holiness.

This chapter, however, focuses on the potential dangers of emotional self-surgery for those with a more traumatic past. If you find in your exploration of self-roles that your compulsions are unusually severe, or if you suspect the presence of a suppressed self-role with suppressed memories, I urge you to get professional help.

We have seen how, with such help, you can expose hidden self-roles and find reconciliation with them. We have seen how suppressed memories can be brought to the surface and processed. We have seen how demonic entities can be identified and expelled.

I hope I have also established that no one can get through these kinds of experiences alone. We were not created to.

9
BREAKING BAD
RELATIONSHIP
HABITS

• • • • • •

Understanding *ourselves means understanding* how we act in relationships. After all, personality roles are nothing but the tools we develop to respond to others.

The concept of personality roles underscores just how complex human relationships are. Just as we relate to others through personality roles, others respond to us through their own personality roles. Each close relationship, then, involves several subrelations between pairs of roles—one in me and one in my partner. To understand how I relate to other people, I have to identify the personality roles they call out in me and vice versa. The obvious complexity of these dynamics helps explain why relationships are such hard work.

This chapter will focus on how understanding our own personality roles can help us improve relationships with those closest to us. To do this, let's return to Ted and May, whom we met back in chapter one.

Married with Children—and Problems

As you recall, Ted and May came to see me for several reasons. First, they disagreed on how to raise their three children. May put great pressure on them to be successful in every way. Ted, on the other hand, spoiled them. He tried to win them over by subtly sabotaging May's plans and rules. Second, they clashed over money matters. Despite their good income, Ted and May were constantly in debt. May handled the finances competently, but Ted used their credit cards freely and blew every budget she established. Then, of course, there was Ted's temper that sometimes inexplicably erupted after a session of ballroom dancing.

Ted and May were concerned and frustrated over these patterns of behavior that they just couldn't seem to break. How had they developed? Where did they come from? How could they change them? Let's go back a bit into their histories to begin to answer these questions.

Ted's mother had been an overwhelmingly competent person. Her one big problem was her husband, who was the original couch potato. She had forged ahead in life, filled with energy and determination. He, by contrast, couldn't compete with others and had never really wanted to. Ted's mother had tried to change his father at first, making plans for him and encouraging action. Harried by her urging, he would try to change, but as soon as she removed the pressure he returned to the couch. Eventually she had given up and decided to carry on without him. She raised their two children, taking a job outside the home as well to cover the extras that Ted's father could not provide from his job as a clerk in a hardware store.

In truth, Ted's father wasn't entirely passive. Knowing his wife despised him, he returned her dislike by purposely sabotaging much that she tried to achieve. It wasn't that he openly opposed her; he was much too dominated by her to try anything that brazen. Instead his resentment showed itself in mean little acts of resistance. If she planned an evening out and forced him to go, he would be late or wear the wrong clothes. He had a genius for identifying pinpricks that would goad her to a fury. Her response was to try to control him all the more fiercely.

Ted and his sister grew up with these parents as the major models for adult roles. Ted developed into the perfect mother's boy. Determined that he would be different from his father, she trained him to do what she wanted from his earliest years, dominating him with her energy and force of personality.

As Ted approached puberty, he began to show little signs of rebellion. His room was no longer tidy, and he never looked neat. It began to appear as if Ted were getting to be "just like his father," which of course infuriated his mother. She redoubled her efforts to make Ted conform, and on the surface she succeeded. Underneath, however, Ted and his father were becoming comrades. Both felt emasculated by her, and both resented it. In response to his parents, Ted developed two ego roles—one passive and submissive, the other bitter and angry. The angry Ted was allowed out very rarely.

May, meanwhile, grew up with a big, hearty, domineering father. As a little girl she was intimated by both his size and his loud voice. He was an alcoholic, and May experienced all the common problems of children in an alcoholic home. She became very submissive—all dark eyes and insecurity.

As time went by, however, her father changed. He became ill; the noise and dash faded. Because he was now dependent on his wife and daughter, he no longer dared to be so aggressive with them. Though passive, he complained constantly in whining tones.

By her late teens May had changed too. When she and her mother took control of the household, all their resentment over years of enforced submission came to the fore. They reversed the old order. Now May's father danced to their tune. May became a dominant, forceful woman; but underneath she still felt insecure and afraid of men.

Just Like Mom

When Ted met May, they felt just right for each other. For both of them, being with the other felt like putting on an old glove molded to their personality. They fit so well, in fact, because each of them was very like the other's opposite-sex parent.

Like all young lovers, Ted and May stayed on their best behavior at first. May was careful not to dominate; Ted acted like a man of action and decision. Yet Ted had been trained to detect insecure and dominant women, and May was a pro at detecting male weakness. So down deep they knew each other's personality types only too well. They took this feeling of comfortable familiarity to be love, and so they married.

Of course when they fell in love none of this was obvious to them; even when they came to talk to me in marital crisis, they still hadn't a clue about why they were acting the way they did. The truth is that we grow up predisposed to choose partners who remind us of our parents. This only makes sense; our own personality roles were, after all, developed to complement those of our parents. Beneath the surface of our rational minds, then, the tendency to seek out familiar personality roles when choosing a mate is always at work, even when we think we are doing the opposite.

A few years into the marriage Ted and May's underlying natures began to show through. Ted became the passive husband that May had determined she would avoid at all costs. May, in her resentment of that, became critical of his ineffectiveness and weakness in every area. As her forcefulness showed through, Ted was unable to match her and surrendered area after area of their family life to her control—also with resentment. Because he didn't feel strong enough to oppose her openly, he sabotaged her in true family tradition, finding subtle, indirect ways to resist her.

That's when they came to see me about raising their children, handling money and dealing with Ted's anger. In each case Ted had found a way to fight back against the domination by May that he resented.

As we have seen, Ted had developed two major roles as he grew up—the submissive mother's boy and the angry young man. May also had developed two personality roles—the strong, forceful woman who despised weakness in men and the submissive girl who was frightened by men. Their relationship was, therefore, no simple Ted-May affair. Instead, each of Ted's roles interacted with each of May's to form four subrelationships. Table 7 illustrates the two personality-role pairs through which May and Ted most commonly related.

May	Ted
Dominant personality role: competent, controlling young woman	Submissive personality role: passive, mother-pleasing boy
Submissive personality role: frightened little girl	Dominant personality role: angry young man

Table 7. Ted and May relate through two personality-role pairs

Here, in a bit more detail, is how the complete set of four subrelationships operated in Ted and May's marriage.

Dominant May, submissive Ted. Competent May plays the same role in Ted's life as his mother did, so Ted responds with his passive mama's-boy style. In this role he shows no initiative and basically follows May's directions. This causes May's competent role to despise him. (She wants a strong Christian husband.) This is represented by the first line in table 7.

Dominant May, dominant Ted. May's contempt brings out the

angry-young-man role in Ted, who remembers all too well receiving contempt from his mother. Most of the time this personality role is suppressed by the mother-pleasing role. This angry role forces Ted into resentful behavior calculated to disturb the mother-pleaser (indulging the children, spending money irresponsibly and so on). Because Ted's angry-young-man role has gained confidence as Ted has been recognized for his professional expertise in the workplace, the mama's-boy has become less able to suppress him. So Ted's angry-young-man role is beginning to respond directly to competent May's contempt in open outbursts of anger.

Submissive May, dominant Ted. When May meets this surprising overt resistance in Ted, she is intimidated; her submissive, frightened-little-girl role appears. This subrelationship makes Ted feel dominant and powerful, reinforcing his desire to express long-suppressed anger in explosions of temper. When faced with May's little-girl role, Ted's angry young man becomes a bully. (This is represented by the lower line in table 7.)

Submissive May, submissive Ted. When his anger dies down, Ted's passive mama's-boy role, appalled at his own behavior, tries to comfort May's little-girl role. He is not good at this, however, and soon she become irritated with his helpless hand-wringing. Dominant May appears once more.

As we can see, Ted and May's relationship is a complex mixture of relationships between their different personality roles. This is why intimate relationships can be so rich and fascinating. Different interactions between different roles go on simultaneously. May's dominant role, for example, may interact on the surface with Ted's submissive role; but beneath the surface her dominant role also interacts with Ted's angry-young-man role. These two interactions are very different. Ted's surface behavior comes from his primary, passive role, and this invokes May's contempt for him. Beneath the surface Ted's angry role picks up her contempt and shares it; he too despises his passive self. The angry Ted resents her contempt, however, as if it were directed at him rather than the passive Ted, because May doesn't consciously distinguish between the two. This heightens Ted's anger and hence his inner tension. Eventually Ted's passive role is unable to keep his angry role submerged, and the angry young man emerges to release his hostility on dominant-competent May.

When angry Ted vents his anger in this way, he faces both dominant May and little-girl May—*but he doesn't know it.* Because competent-dominant May retains a streak of insecurity from her early interactions with her father, she quickly submerges and leaves little-girl May to face Ted. Ted, however, still thinks he is facing the competent-dominant May; hence when May responds submissively, it rewards his bullying tactics and encourages his violent behavior.

Ted and May didn't always interact like this. Ted's angry-young-man role sometimes emerged when his masculinity was encouraged rather than despised, as when they went ballroom dancing and he was allowed to lead. Under these circumstances Ted's young-man role was very attractive to both sides of May. Then her competent role enjoyed and appreciated his skill as a partner while her little-girl self enjoyed his leadership. This pattern experienced in ballroom dancing showed us how their relationship could be made much more healthy in the future.

Helping Ted and May
Once they understood each other's personality-role structures, May and Ted both felt relieved. Neither of them liked what was happening to them, and simply understanding it brought a great sense of hope. For several weeks they each kept a diary of their interactions and compared notes when they were with me. Soon they were able to see the changes in each of them as they occurred and to recognize which personality role was "out" in themselves and each other. They were getting to know each other. But this by itself did not change their actions. Angry scenes

and antagonistic behavior still occurred.

Hostility between their respective roles lay at the root of these problems. For improving these relationships between May's and Ted's roles, the same principle I use to help individuals reconcile personality roles applies: mutual hostility must give way to mutual appreciation. The hostility between May's forceful self and Ted's passive self, for example, was not unlike angry Ted's dislike for his own passive side.

Overcoming hostilities between personality roles in a relationship involves the slow process of relearning habits. Forceful May set herself the goal of doing for Ted what his mother never did—encouraging his masculinity. She saw that passive Ted had been prevented from growing into a man. Over time she learned to honor Ted's masculinity in a variety of ways: she stopped ordering him about like a child; she learned to suggest and ask; she learned to reward him for being assertive. Her dancing style had to become more pervasive in her life.

May was a very creative woman who made rapid progress—but it was not easy. The habit of constant command was hard to overcome. She was committed to Ted, however, and understanding his internal struggle helped. She now had specific goals for their relationship.

This change meant that May had to encourage the forceful angry-young-man role in Ted to be more prominent. At first this felt like encouraging Ted's anger, which she naturally resisted. But she came to see that the angry-young-man role did not always have to be angry. She came to understand that certain circumstances had made him angry and that those circumstances could be changed.

Releasing this anger required a major effort from Ted's passive self, who feared the angry-young-man role too. Deliberately allowing him "out," in fact, was as hard for Ted as it was for May. But Ted's passive side learned to appreciate the forceful aspect of Ted's young man and understand the reasons for his anger.

With competent May's encouragement, he began to explore his emerging masculinity and to enjoy it without anger.

The angry Ted played a key role in Ted's change. One day he emerged as we were talking about a previous temper tantrum. Angrily he expressed his frustration with himself. He said he bullied May because he was "addicted to power"; he said he was ashamed of his attitude. He admitted that the anger he was acting out was really directed at his mother. Finally, as we prayed about this anger, he experienced a spiritual breakthrough. He was able to release his anger and forgive his mother.

Not surprisingly, this led to changes in the way Ted related to his mother as a middle-aged adult. Until now he had continued to act submissively around her. Now he began to be more asser-tive by letting his young-man role out. May worked with him as a supporter and encourager.

May too was changing during the counseling process. She was learning to trust her inner little girl's ability to encourage and support Ted. This was not to say that she swung to the other extreme, becoming Ted's subordinate rather than an equal partner. Rather, it meant that the tender side of her nature was no longer despised as weak. As Ted's young man encouraged the emergence of this side of May, a new sense of wholeness and inner peace flowered in her. Her two sides began to appreciate rather than dislike each other.

As you can see, the changes that both Ted and May needed to achieve greater *internal* unity and defuse *internal* hostilities were the same as those needed to improve their *relationship*. Working on understanding and integrating roles with a partner gives both people an advantage over the person who goes it alone: they can support and encourage one another.

Earlier we saw that when a person is told that hostility between the parts of himself must be replaced by trust and appreciation, he fears the change. Exactly the same dynamic occurs when one is trying to improve relationships. It felt quite wrong to the dominant May to encourage Ted's young man. It seemed to Ted's passive self that encouraging May's little girl left him with a responsibility he could not bear. Yet these changes were necessary. Faith played a crucial role here. Each party believed that, because of Christ, they could change. Each of them genuinely wanted to end their unloving behavior—not only because it hurt them but also because it hurt God.

Eventually they learned new patterns of behavior. I want to emphasize that this did not mean that the roles simply reversed, with a dominant Ted controlling a passive May. Instead, a much richer relational pattern developed, with mutual respect and appreciation for all parts of their personalities. There are still times when competent May manages some part of their lives; she's good at budgeting, for example, and still looks after their finances. The difference is that Ted now not only agrees to her leadership but appreciates it. As a result, he no longer feels the need to undermine her efforts. On the other hand, May loves Ted's forceful role now because he is no longer angry. The gentle, playful side of May (her little girl, still tender but no longer frightened) now brings out the indulgent, playful side of Ted (his little boy, who's compliant but no longer passive). A whole new part of their relationship has developed. And they're having a lot of fun.

What's Normal?

After the many dysfunctional relationships I have described in this book, I may have given the gloomy impression that under the surface, everyone has major problems relating to everyone else. This is not the case. What is true, however, is that every relationship, no matter how healthy or dysfunctional, does involve a complex interaction of personality roles. Consider the case of George and Phyllis.

George was a strong emotional resource for his young family. He had been a bulwark of protection and support for a long time as his wife first worked through problems stemming from a difficult childhood and then suffered a miscarriage.

When George's father died, he and Phyllis quite suddenly—and quite easily—both changed roles. The night his father died George wept like a baby in Phyllis's arms. She found she could play the comforting role of mother for a man who had often been her protection in the moments of her own childlike fear and sadness. During the difficult months that followed, she drew on deep strength she had forgotten she possessed. She explored a whole new side of her personality and became a more rounded, complete person as a result.

It does not necessarily take a trauma like this to bring out alternative personality roles in a relationship. Greg and Paula, for example, are often both very serious and intense people; but when in the evening a different side of Paula comes out to play—say, a playful or sexual side—she may be able to coax out a different side of Greg. As a result they experience a new sense of delight in their married life. This kind of role-changing in a relationship is good and healthy.

Remember, our one model of total emotional wholeness is Jesus, who moved easily between rebuking the disciples for their unbelief and offering them comfort and support. You too can have a set of personality roles that interact smoothly to foster healthy, godly relationships.

Improving Your Relationships

Even if you are not married, you can still learn a great deal from Ted and May's experience. The approach they took to improving their relationship can work with parents, bosses, friends and colleagues. You can begin to understand why you and others react to each other the way you do, which is the first step toward improving a relationship.

The process begins with the type of self-analysis we discussed in chapter six. When you have a good sense of the personality roles you developed during childhood and have carried into adult life, you can begin to explore how they figure in your current relationships. Write down your personality roles on a worksheet such as the one in table 8 below.

Relationship	Personality Role Characteristics	Experiences
With opposite-sex parent		
With authority figures		
With opposite sex now		

Table 8. A relationship worksheet

First, consider your interactions with authority figures. How does each of your personality roles react? It is common for us to develop submissive-dominant role pairs. The key question is how submissive or how dominant we will be in any given situation. We all need to submit to authority figures sometimes, and most of us need to take the lead with them sometimes. Are you comfortable playing both roles, or does one of them invoke internal tension? May and Ted eventually found a balance between roles so that each could comfortably alternate between leading and following as necessary.

If you intensely dislike surrendering control or assuming control even when it's appropriate, chances are that somewhere inside you a disliked personality role possesses the skills you need. Try to identify that personality role, and seek to understand why it is disliked. What were the childhood experiences that led to its suppression?

Second, explore your relationships with the opposite sex and the same sex. We often play different roles depending on the sex of the company in which we find ourselves. Do you use a different personality role when with men or women? If so, what are its characteristics? How is it related to previously identified dominant and submissive roles? Are you much more comfortable with one sex than with the other?

Usually we learn sex roles from our parents. The same-sex parent typically becomes our model, while the other parent becomes a teacher and sounding board. Both parents are influential from the start, but modeling our same-sex parent is particularly important in the years before puberty, while developing a relationship with our other parent becomes important around puberty. If you had a poor or missing relationship with one or both parents, how did you cope? Is part of your gender identity kept submerged? Did you have to struggle to emerge into adulthood?

All these questions are intended to uncover whether there is fear or hostility between your different personality roles. Where such fear or hostility occurs, I become uncomfortable playing one of my roles. I then begin to avoid situations where that personality role should emerge. For example, a man brought up in a home where anger is unacceptable may suppress the forceful side of his nature, because that's where his anger resides. He may avoid all confrontations because they might bring out his suppressed forceful role. This gives rise to unhealthy patterns of people-pleasing on the one hand and of dominance and anger on the other.

If this particular form of division plays into our sexuality, we develop unhealthy and unchristian sexual tendencies. One mild-mannered young man who had experienced sexual abuse as a child rejected his anger and his sexuality altogether. When this suppressed role "took over," he became involved in sadistic sexual relations with other men. Conversely, the suppressed sexuality may be associated with passivity and the victim role.

Are you very different in a group from the way you are with

one other person? Are you comfortable in emotional settings? Which personality role takes the lead in these different environments? Once again, you are looking for settings in which internal tension reveals itself. It is normal to play different roles with different skills. What matters is whether you experience an inner sense of equilibrium.

Thinking about situations that cause inner tension can help us identify roles that are rejected or disliked—which will in turn help us understand what we need to change to improve our relationships. If you find, for example, that you have suppressed your more forceful role, try to develop relationships where that role is given an opportunity to express itself. Church can be an ideal setting for this. In a Bible study you might choose to speak up more and express yourself. You might learn how to disagree in love. If you talk with a trusted group of friends about what you are doing, they can help. The very act of sharing your struggle, in fact, will become part of your growth. As the forceful role gets practice, you will become able to confront others appropriately in other places, such as at home or in the workplace.

Choosing a Mate
The Bible's standards are often in conflict with society's norms, but nowhere is this more sharply felt than in premarital behavior.

For starters, the Bible insists that romantic love isn't everything: Christians are not to choose an unbelieving partner, even if they find themselves falling in love with him or her. Second, the Bible insists that sexual intercourse is for marriage only. Finally, while our culture would have us believe that romantic love can conquer all, the Bible paints a picture of dysfunctional family patterns being reproduced in troubled marriages. Take the descendants of Sarah and Abraham. The trouble begins when Abraham, fearful that another man will kill him to get his beautiful wife, Sarah, lies (and persuades her to lie) about their marital status (see Genesis 12 and 20). This dishonesty repeats itself in the marriage of their son Isaac and his wife Rebecca (see Genesis 26). The dishonesty that Rebecca learns she teaches to her son Jacob as she manipulates him into deceiving his father (Genesis 27:5-6). Jacob in turn marries not one but two wives who, along with him, maintain the family tradition of deceit, manipulation and control (see Genesis 31).

The warning is clear: if we have not understood a dysfunctional family pattern and grown out of it, we are likely to repeat it by choosing a mate who will help us do so. Ted and May illustrate the point perfectly. What feels like love may actually be only a familiar fit. If the fit is dysfunctional, then the relationship is predestined for trouble.

I remember talking to a woman who had just experienced her third divorce. Each husband had been an alcoholic, as had her father. Her explanation was that she had been deceived by each husband. I didn't believe that. Having grown up in an alcoholic home, she was, at least unconsciously, an expert at detecting alcoholic personalities. She also knew how to get on with alcoholic men. Men who weren't alcoholics, in fact, made her uncomfortable; they didn't behave the way she expected. Because her interaction with the opposite sex had been conditioned by her interaction with her father, her roles had developed to fit his.

To avoid picking out a mate who will help you repeat dysfunctional patterns, you must know yourself and be growing. Study your parents' marriage for clues to potential dangers. Find out all you can about your grandparents' marriages too. Do you see any patterns? By now you should have a good idea of your own personality-role structure. How does it set you up for a possible disaster?

If you are seriously dating or actually engaged to someone, explore your patterns of behavior with your prospective spouse. If you had a poor relationship with your parent of the opposite sex, ask yourself if your fiancé is in any way like that parent. Since you, like the woman who kept marrying alcoholics, may be heavily defended against seeing similarities between your parent and your fiancé, ask some people who know both parties for their opinions. If your fiancé *is* like your parent in some important ways, that doesn't necessarily mean you should not marry. What it does mean is that some hard work is in order before the wedding. The process that May and Ted went through can serve as a model for engaged couples too.

Marriage Is Work

God created marriage to be an especially effective way for people to grow emotionally. Whenever two people are determined to make marriage work, it can work; but it is not easy. A satisfying lifelong relationship is the result of a lifetime of work at unselfishness.

As we have seen, all this is complicated, because a marriage is not just a relationship between two people; it is also a set of relationships between their roles. In addition to making a commitment to personal growth toward unselfishness, then, a Christian who wants to make marriage work must be willing to explore her nature deeply with her spouse, who knows her better than anyone else. To do this, she must get to know the structure of her own personality roles.

The problems in a marriage are the sum total of both individuals' problems; working at marriage is simply working at my problems and helping my spouse work with hers. That is why marriage is the ideal setting for growth.

The pattern of growth that begins by identifying personality roles, reviewed above in the case study of Ted and May, is now familiar to you. As I suggested to May and Ted, keeping separate diaries in which you record your impressions about the interactions between your respective roles is a good way to identify the dynamics that make your marriage what it is. Talking about these dynamics is essential. Asking each other questions just after a time of conflict can be very helpful in clarifying what really happened.

I don't mean to imply that this process will necessarily go smoothly. Sometimes anger and resentment spill out during discussions about relational dynamics. Also, new tools of any kind—even a tool intended to enhance mutual understanding, such as the concept of personality roles—can be used as weapons. Be careful not to use your personality-role understanding as a means of attack when you are angry. That's how marriages are destroyed.

If you discover problems in your marriage that feel bigger than the two of you, get help. Just understanding how personality roles interact is not sufficient to solve all the kinds of conflicts a couple may face.

Raising Children

The more we understand how our own personality roles developed, the more demanding parenting seems. As we have seen, we parents are the principal agents that God uses to develop our children's personality-role structures. The more we are at peace with our own roles, the more we are able to move between them appropriately—and the healthier it is for our children. As we parents play our different roles over the years, our kids become adept at responding to these different versions of Dad and Mommy. Their varying responses cluster into different personality roles in them.

You may recall from earlier chapters that if a parent's personality roles are hostile to each other, they create mirror tensions in the child, who is forced to try to relate to two mutually hostile versions of one parent. Children happily cope with differences in us at different times, but if those differences demand incompatible behavior, then there is trouble.

Suppose, for example, that an "angry Daddy" role demands absolute submission and fiercely punishes any deviation from it. Later, in a more gentle personality role, the same father expects his child to be loving and playful. In other words, what is punished by one personality role is rewarded by another. The injustice of this generates anger in the child.

Because children tend to accept parental behavior as a given and blame themselves for tensions, the resentment of a parental role is transferred to a suppressed internal personality role. The angry-father role generates a submissive personality role in his child, while the playful-father role generates an assertive role in the child. The submissive role is then despised by the child as the *cause* of Daddy's anger. In this way the anger is internalized by the next generation.

For me as a parent, the key to avoiding this problem is to be at ease with myself in all my roles. After all, the essence of a healthy personality is to be comfortable behaving differently in different roles. Because I accept this dynamic in myself, it becomes acceptable to me that my child behaves differently in different situations too. This acceptance allows him to feel approved in all his differing roles.

When disciplining a child for inappropriate behavior, it is important to distinguish between acts that are always wrong and acts that are merely out of place in certain situations. In the latter case a child is merely working in the wrong role, while in the former case a role is behaving wrongly.

Suppose a mother teaches her daughter that lying is always wrong and disciplines her along those lines. If she then turns around and requires her to lie in a certain situation—say, to protect her image in front of a friend—the child becomes understandably confused, and a personality-role conflict may begin.

In contrast, a mother who enjoys laughing with her daughter may nevertheless punish her for laughing at cruelty and pain. As long as she is consistent about her overall message—that laughter is good *sometimes*—the girl's serious and playful sides will coexist without tension. In that case the child is on the road to a healthy acceptance of her differing personality roles.

10
BLAMING, CHOOSING AND RESPONSIBILITY

• • • • • •

Sarah was *beautiful, and that had made her power-*
ful. She was used to being treated preferentially by men, as beautiful women often are.

Overall, hers was a charmed life. Married to a financially successful business leader who provided her with servants and other
luxuries, she felt she lacked only one thing: a baby. After years
of unsuccessfully trying for a child, she arranged for a surrogate
mother to bear her husband's child. The arrangement was con-
venient; the woman she approached about it was a servant in
their home. Several years after the woman had borne the couple
a child, Sarah got into a jealous rage and demanded her husband
send the servant and her child away. Though agonizing over the
injustice of the demand, Sarah's husband responded as he always
did. He let his wife have her way.

You see, in spite of his many successes out in the business

world, Sarah's husband was insecure about his marriage; he feared losing his extraordinarily beautiful wife to another man. To keep his wife close to him, he would take her along on his business travels. When Sarah was with him, however, he would often fear rousing the jealousy of his business associates so much that he would pretend—and get her to pretend—that they were not married. The situation was bizarre. Twice Sarah found herself actually being courted by her husband's powerful business associates before he would own up to the truth!

Sound too contrived to be true? Read the story for yourself in Genesis 12, 16 and 20. The husband I have been talking about is Abraham—that strange mixture of brave warrior and cowardly husband.

Sharing an Addiction

Nowadays we might describe a couple like Sarah and Abraham as "codependent."[1] A codependent relationship is one in which both parties reinforce each other's addictive or compulsive behavior. While alcoholics, for example, are addicted to alcohol, their codependent partners are addicted to feeling needed by them. Thus the alcoholic compulsively drinks and the codependent partner compulsively covers up for her, making it possible for the alcoholic to continue her addiction. Although the codependent partner might not realize or admit it, he as much as the alcoholic needs the primary addiction in place to feel good. As we have observed before, such compulsive behavior reveals the presence of a suppressed personality role in both parties.

Why do I say that Sarah and Abraham's relationship smacks of codependency? In the first place, Abraham's fearfulness and dishonesty seems to me like compulsive, rather than rational, behavior. As far as we know, Sarah had never given him reason to believe that he couldn't successfully keep her for himself; nor had any of his male peers tried to take her away. Second, Sarah was inexplicably willing to cooperate with Abraham's compulsive dishonesty, which made it possible for him to repeat it. Although she may have told herself that she was simply being a supportive, loving wife, she was, in fact, enabling her husband to continue his dishonesty.

But what kind of need could Sarah have been getting met by supporting Abraham that way? We might imagine that she went along with Abraham's schemes because she felt a nagging sense of guilt for being a burden: if she were not cursed with such unusual beauty, her husband would not be so fearful and scheming. In that scenario Abraham's problem became Sarah's problem. I suspect her barrenness made her insecure too, so that she was willing to accept reassurance from the admiration of other men, even while she remained submissive to her husband. Thus playing along with, rather than resisting, Abraham's insecure behavior may have made Sarah feel wanted and desirable too (and thus powerful). If so, encouraging Abraham's weakness was necessary to fan her own sense of well-being. The idea that she caused his problem by being too beautiful, of course, was nonsense; Abraham's irrational insecurity and compulsive dishonesty were his problem, not Sarah's.

In the last chapter we traced the interaction between the different personality roles in a marriage relationship. The same role dynamics occur in a codependent marriage, except for an added twist. Codependents assist in their family's destruction under the illusion that they are doing just the opposite.

Codependency has tragic consequences. God intervened to save Sarah, but he does not always do so. Codependents often attach themselves over and over again to the most damaging partners they can find and then implicitly encourage their behavior despite excruciating stress. As a result, the partner's problem grows worse. Codependents are convinced that they are helpless to change their situation because life has trained them for the victim role. As professional victims, they are tragedies waiting to happen.

People who are fully codependent display at least four characteristics: they are addicted to approval; they submit to abuse to gain the approval; they wrongly blame themselves for others' problems; and they are controlled by others' decisions.

My interpretation of the Sarah-Abraham saga illustrates how these characteristics can get played out. It was abusive of Abraham to involve Sarah in his compulsion and to blame her beauty for it. Sarah took the blame because she needed to be needed. As a result, her life was not controlled by her own choices but by Abraham's.

Let's examine how these four aspects of codependency have been played out in a more modern—and, in the end, a more tragic—family situation.

Who's to Blame?

Cindy grew up in a small town in the Bible Belt, where women were expected to stand by their men under all circumstances. That was exactly the way her mother had lived.

Cindy's mother, Margaret, was an interesting woman. She had studied to be a nurse, but gave up her career when she fell in love with a handsome farmer's son who seduced her one weekend when he was up visiting friends. Starry-eyed, Margaret followed him back to his hometown, and within three weeks they were married. Only then did she realize what life was going to be like for the balance of her years.

Her husband, John, had inherited his farm from his parents two years before, and running it took all his time and energy. As his wife, Margaret was expected to work just as hard in the kitchen and in the chicken run. Life was hard, but she never complained.

When John grew angry at his disappointments with the farm, he vented his frustration on his wife by physically abusing her. Still, she never complained. She learned to cover her bruises with makeup when she went to town, but she couldn't help but wince when she lifted a bag of groceries on a bruised arm. Eventually people figured out what was happening. Unfortunately nobody considered it their business to intervene; such situations, after all, are common. A few understanding women befriended the battered wife and shared her burdens as best they could.

Little Cindy was John's pride and joy, but even with her he was unable to control his fits of anger. One day she tried, in her childlike way, to stop him from beating her mother. One backhanded blow flung her against the wall. John was bitterly sorry. Gathering his little girl in his arms, he apologized and told her he didn't mean it. But she had already learned her lesson. From then on, she turned a silent face to the wall when her mother was beaten, suppressing the part of her that cried out at the injustice. She had learned that intervening was a punishable offense; her father demanded total submission.

So a division began to form in little Cindy's mind. The angry role began to split away and be buried deep inside—unacceptable, unwanted, unacknowledged. From then on the victim role took control of her life.

Cindy felt that she could save her mother by keeping Daddy happy, so she worked incessantly to please him. She made sure his slippers were out by the fire and his coffee ready as he came in. Her whole life, in fact, became an effort to please him. When her father beat her mother, Cindy assumed she had not been good enough; the rebellious person within her that abhorred her father's behavior must have slipped out and made him angry. So Cindy grew up codependent and highly proficient at keeping an angry man calm—at least some of the time.

Deep inside, meanwhile, a little Cindy remained ignored in the darkness. She knew that her father's behavior was unjust, unfair and *wrong*. Over the years this inner Cindy cherished a bitter anger at her outer victim role. This only convinced the outer Cindy, however, that she was wicked inside and needed to keep her angry self down.

Years later, Cindy also married a man named John. He was a

lay preacher who began Bible school to prepare for full-time ministry a year after they got married. Naturally Cindy had picked a man with a violent streak; it was the only kind of man she knew how to handle.

Even at Bible school, where John had gained quite a reputation as a promising preacher, he would lose his temper and hit her. Cindy had so well internalized a victim mindset as a child that she never even considered that her husband might be to blame for his behavior. She went to the school counselor to ask him what *she* was doing wrong!

The counselor, in turn, made matters worse. Embarrassed by the information—John was, after all, the school's star student—the counselor suggested Cindy avoid making her husband angry and be more submissive. For ten miserable years after that, Cindy continued to endure physical abuse. Like her mother, she never complained. But one day she ran away, unable to take it anymore.

Cindy's story illustrates how a codependent's fundamental characteristics work together to destroy her. As a child Cindy was trained to hunger for a love that never came, and she was willing to pay any price to get it. She had come to believe that she deserved the bad things that happened to her. And she felt helpless to make her own decisions.

Perhaps even more strikingly, Cindy's story illustrates how codependents are conditioned to feel responsible for the actions of others. Cindy believed she could stop her father's violence by being a very good girl. Later, the Bible-school counselor made her feel that she could stop her husband's violence by being a very good wife. Cindy's church often gave her the same message. She was told in many different ways that she was responsible for her husband's decisions; it was her support that would enable him to meet the demands of Christian leadership. While the abuse was going on, he was publicly honored, first as a student and later as a pastor. The message she got was clear: "There's obviously nothing wrong with John. The abuse is your fault."

I chose to use a case of family violence to illustrate codependency, but it can take many different forms. An emotionally distant parent can induce this same unhealthy sense of guilt in a child: "It's my own fault that Daddy doesn't love me. I must try harder to be good." A perfectionist parent and a punitive, critical parent can also have this effect.

Learning to Be a Victim

As we have seen, codependent people feel worthless. Their determination to satisfy others' needs comes from an aching hunger for love and approval.

Children were created by God to be in relationship with others. But that marvelous ability to love becomes a terrible hunger when it is not returned. Children instinctively keep looking for the affection they have been denied. Trying to please the ones who reject them, they suppress the inner angry self and appease aggressors. Such people are set up to become victimized later in life. That is why Cindy ended up marrying John. Cindy's father had trained her to yield herself to violent men and blame herself for their abuse. The personality role that could have protested was buried deeper with each abusive incident.

Heidi Vanderbilt offers this description of the way sexual abuse prepares the victim for further abuse:

Sexually abused children teach themselves to endure assault. Instead of learning to protect themselves, they learn that they *can't* protect themselves. As adults they can be blind to anger others would find obvious. They may freeze or go limp when threatened. Someone who has never been abused can say no, can walk or run away, can scream and fight. The incest victim often doesn't know what to do except to wait for the danger to be over.

Child incest victims often become adult rape victims. Almost one quarter of the incest victims Mary W. Armsworth studied went on to be sexually abused by their therapists.[2] Many incest victims as adults chose abusive partners.

Judy, who was abused from infancy by her grandmother, grew up with what she describes as free-floating feelings of shame. "I always felt there was something wrong about me," she says, "something loathsome."

She married a violent man. She believed that when he beat her it was her fault and what she deserved. She believed the beatings were a sign of his love. She stayed with him for more than a decade, leaving him only when she became afraid that her suicidal feelings would overwhelm her and that she would die, leaving her child alone and in danger from his father.[3]

Sexual and physical abuse are effective ways to train a child to be a victim, but they are not the only methods. Any parenting that produces a sense of worthlessness can have the same effect. Constant criticism, belittling, neglect, emotional withdrawal—in fact, anything that creates the impression that children are not loved—will have a similar result.

The Anger Within

Part of the victims' dilemma is what to do with the anger they feel. This may seem surprising, because they often appear resigned rather than angry when the victim role is in control. The suppressed assertive role, however, contains their anger at the injustices they've suffered. As we have seen, this splitting off of emotion is God's built-in defense mechanism to prevent the child from being overwhelmed by his feelings.

Victimized children learn that the anger within them is dangerous; if they express it, they may lose whatever signs of love their parents do show them. Typically, parents of such children reinforce this by sending the message that anger is a sign of rebellion that must be punished. Children treated this way learn to hate, fear and reject their angry role. They come to believe that their abuse is the punishment for their anger rather than its cause. Thus the external rejection by the parent is reinforced by the child herself: "I am a bad, angry girl, and that is why Mommy hits me."

In time this dynamic causes the now-adult child to believe other abusers who tell her how worthless and deserving of punishment she is. At this point the anger may be so hidden beneath layers of hopelessness—despair of ever deserving someone's love—that it never surfaces. The victim simply trudges on from tragedy to tragedy, unsurprised by each one.

If you fit these descriptions of people with a victim mentality, you need to discover your angry role and validate its outrage at the abuse you suffered. You must welcome the inner victim with compassion and understanding into your circle of selfhood. Then and only then can you begin your healing process and learn how to stop playing the victim role.

Establishing Boundaries

Early in childhood children naturally assume that the world revolves round them. It is natural for them to think that things happen because of their decisions. In normal development they grow to realize that many things are outside their control; in psychological terms, they discover their boundary. Inside the boundary is their sphere of influence, where they make decisions and are responsible for the consequences. Outside the boundary they may have some influence over events, but not ultimate responsibility.

At first all parents treat their children as extensions of themselves, making their decisions for them. Because newborn babies are not capable of making decisions, this is inevitable. As they grow, however, children begin to make more and more important choices. This decision-making means that the child is taking control of some area of his life. Slowly a boundary is established between mother and child as he learns what he can control and what his parent must control. Within the boundary is his territory, where he learns the consequences of making good and bad decisions. A child's sense of self, of boundaries and of his ability to make decisions, therefore, are tightly connected.

A child learns that the area under his control defines him as a person in his community. This process begins very early as he learns to control his own body functions—eating, going to the bathroom, dressing and so on. With control comes responsibility: he is expected to use his control in order to function in his community. As his control of his body and then his environment expands, more is expected of him by the community; as he rises to those expectations, he is considered more adult.

Take the simple task of eating. At six months the child doesn't control his food; it gets all over him. Later he learns to feed himself, first with his hands and then with utensils. His control over the eating process is conditioned at each stage by the expectations of others. In other words, what is acceptable dinner-table behavior in a one-year-old is usually frowned on in a two-year-old and expressly forbidden in a five-year-old.

This process of gaining others' approval is accompanied by the child's growing sense of becoming an independent person. This in turn triggers a desire for more control, and so the process continues. As he grows, he also learns what is outside his control, or what we might call his self-boundary. Things outside this boundary are not his responsibility.

As this process unfolds, parents typically experience a sense of loss. Baby no longer needs them as much. This can introduce stress into the relationship as parents and children fight a tug-of-war for control. Small children constantly assert their will to determine what lies inside and outside their boundary. At four a child may refuse to eat broccoli; at fourteen she may insist on decorating her room with rock-and-roll posters; at twenty she may choose to date someone her parents don't like. At every stage the child is testing the limits of parental authority. Needless to say, this process can be very trying for parents—especially insecure parents who *like* to keep children dependent on them. Typically, insecure parents strongly resist their children's assertions of independence, especially in its later stages. Most parents want their children to be toilet-trained. Many find it harder to relinquish control of the car.

In severe cases like Cindy's, punishment may be used to stop the growth process altogether. As a result, the decision-making part of Cindy's personality was deadened. Personality traits associated with decision-making and self-assertion split off as an unwanted personality role. The compliant role thought of itself as the whole self, treating the decisive personality role as *other*, as something lying beyond its boundary. We have seen how this created a "helpless victim" mentality in Cindy.

Pia Mellody, a self-confessed recovering codependent, has described the difficulty she used to have in making the simplest decisions. When her husband complained that she left all the lights on in their house, for instance, the compliant Pia became afraid to turn them on at all. He came home one evening to find her using the bathroom in the dark. When he asked her to be more moderate, she had no idea how to decide which lights to leave on and which to leave off. Forced to make a decision, she finally counted the number of lights in the house and divided by three: this many lights and only this many, she decided, could she leave on at any given time.[4] Such are the struggles of the recovering codependent.

When children grow up with no ability to decide anything for themselves, they look for authority figures to tell them what to do. They seek to replace the suppressed decision-making self with another person; they attempt, in fact, to incorporate the decision-making other into the self to compensate for their own lost inner self.

There are many authority figures ready to exploit such people. Some men, for example, are only too willing to take control of a woman's decisions about her sex life. Bosses, church leaders and even therapists themselves may take advantage of a victim's pliability.

When Cindy came to me for help, she wanted me—the authority figure—to tell her what to do. Although it can be appropriate for pastors to give direction, it was important that I not become another decision-maker for Cindy. She had to take responsibility for herself. We looked at Scripture together. I even helped her to think through different options and their consequences. But I refused to tell her what to do. In the end, she made her own decision. Though I had fully informed and supported her during the decision-making process, she had nonetheless clearly taken control. I was proud of her. She was growing up.

Abused children have problems with boundaries in many other ways besides decision-making. Some learn to make decisions that reflect false notions about the self. Remember Judy, the little girl abused by her grandmother? When her caregiver became her abuser, Judy learned that her body and her sexuality were controlled by more powerful others. As an adult, therefore, she compulsively surrendered her body to anyone who asked. Incest victims like Judy are taught in the most graphic way that they are *open:* they have no physical or sexual boundaries.

Absence of boundaries produces a loss of personhood. Events have the child in a fatal grip from which there seems to be no escape. He is forced to look to others for help, yet instinctively gravitates toward new victimizers. When these victimizers make bad decisions for him, the codependent person takes all the blame. Because they have no boundaries, other people's mistakes are theirs too.

Codependents are caught in a terribly difficult dilemma. They feel out of control, and in fact they are. Others pull the strings of their lives, making their decisions and rendering them powerless. They feel their only hope is to influence others to be nice to them, so that they will make decisions that help them. People-pleasing behavior becomes a way of life, an effort to control a runaway existence.

Are you compelled to do whatever is necessary to avoid the

anger of others? Do you find honest confrontation impossible? Are most of your decisions controlled by others in one way or another? If you find yourself answering yes to any of these questions, you may well be struggling with codependency. Even successful leaders like Abraham who appear strong to others are not immune. If virtually all your decisions are based on keeping others happy, you can still be codependent.

But there is hope. The next chapter explores the resources available to Christians who struggle with a confused sense of responsibility.

11
PLEASING PEOPLE, PLEASING GOD

• • • • • • •

Religious *codependents make wonderful parishion-*
ers. They trust religious leaders fully. They work hard and serve
endlessly. They are so happy to be given direction that they will
do almost anything.

The trouble is that they are not working for the right reasons—
or even the right person. Often God is not the one they are trying
to please.

Mrs. Jones was a devoted worker at her church; she faithfully
arranged flowers every week, and everyone admired her devotion
to that duty. One day Mary Smith wanted to do the flowers in
memory of her mother. That seemed reasonable to the pastor,
who readily agreed; but Mrs. Jones was devastated and went into
a depression. Her strong reaction came because arranging flowers
satisfied a need to be needed, and Mary's offer exposed the fact
that she was not indispensable.

Mrs. Jones's response revealed that her motive was not as unselfish as appearances suggested. As a codependent Christian, she was attempting to satisfy an inner need for approval. Her driving motive was self-oriented.

In the last chapter I discussed why codependents seek out authority figures to make decisions for them. This often appeals to leaders who want faithful followers—including leaders in the church—but it is wrong. You cannot grow into Christian maturity if you have surrendered your will to a pastor or teacher, because then you are choosing to follow other people rather than God. God holds *you* responsible for your life, and that means making your own informed decisions.

Pastors and teachers who make a codependent's choices for him continue the abuse that caused the codependency. The Bible speaks with authority, and so should preachers of the Word—but even as Jesus respects our God-given right to say no to him, so should those who speak in his name.

Turning to God

God is the ultimate authority figure. Not surprisingly, then, codependents are often drawn to him as their final hope in the search for someone to make them whole. Though God does delight in making us whole, he insists that we actively participate in the process. In other words, he never cooperates with our efforts to suppress parts of ourselves, including our assertive selves. He created us and has a perfect vision of what we could be like if we developed every part of our personality. This is another way of saying that he loves us.

The Christian who has suppressed an assertive role and cultivated a compliant-victim role faces special problems relating to such a God. To help the codependent believer grow in wholeness, God eventually makes her uncomfortable with her relational patterns. But this is not at all what codependent Christians are seeking. They don't want emotional growth into a healthy sense of selfhood—they want to be controlled.

The kind of Christianity codependents do feel comfortable with is flawed in at least two ways. First, the codependent Christian recognizes his sinfulness and longs to submit to God's will—so far so good. But because he lacks an appropriate sense of boundaries, he longs to completely abandon his own will at the same time. God will not become enmeshed with us, however; his boundaries are clear. He loves us, lets us know his will and requires that we *choose* to follow him freely, because he respects us. He expects us to live with the consequences of our choice like responsible adults. As my friend Jill Briscoe says, "God doesn't want jellyfish—not even *evangelly*fish." He offers us an honest, open relationship with him, and that is exactly what the codependent cannot face.

It is a false Christianity, then, that allows us to think we can stop making decisions. Becoming a Christian actually requires us to make more decisions, because God makes us into his own trusted children: "Because you are sons, God sent the Spirit of his Son into our hearts, the Spirit who calls out, '*Abba*, Father.' So you are no longer a slave, but a son; and since you are a son, God has made you also an heir" (Galatians 4:6-7). I will say more about Christian decision-making later, but for now I'll summarize the main point so far: *Many Christians attempt to enmesh with God to avoid decision-making. This leads to legalism and disappointment with God.*

Second, the eager-to-please Christian earnestly does God's will but often looks for something in return. She believes that if she is a "good child" for her heavenly Father, God will be obligated to satisfy her need for love. Such thinking is not compatible with true Christianity, which is built on God's free, unconditional love. Grace—God's generous acceptance of us when we don't deserve it—is not understood by codependents. Because their whole existence is based on *earning* favor, to receive it freely is hard for them.

When God does not satisfy their expectations, such Christians project onto him the problems they experienced with parents. They may perceive God as angry or remote and needing to be placated. When something bad happens, they leap quickly to the conclusion that it was a judgment on them for being bad. They heap on punishment and belittle themselves, moving into the victim role.

On the surface their self-criticism may seem like humility. What they are expressing, however, is actually self-hate. The distinction is important, for if we approve of the codependent's "humility," we are really agreeing with his opinion that he is worthless. Such is the perverted logic of the codependent victim. A glance at church history shows that this is nothing new. Medieval monks wearing hair shirts, beating themselves with whips and starving their bodies are only the more obvious examples.

True humility means that I must accept God's goodness to me. Recognizing that I don't deserve it, I enter into it fully. I rejoice in it, for joy is the hallmark of true humility. Fearful doubts about God's acceptance of me expose the legalistic mindset of the victim role.

But Isn't This Love?

Codependent Christians appear very loving. They pour them-selves out, going to extraordinary lengths to serve others. They hear about Jesus washing the disciples' feet and offering his life for the sins of others and immediately feel on familiar territory. Female people-pleasers who are married read Paul's command to submit to husbands and conclude that their codependency is Christian.

The confusion is understandable. Dying to self *is* fundamental to Christianity, and codependents take that to mean they should lose themselves in others and in God.

But there are important differences between codependent be-havior and true Christian love. First, true Christian love serves the best interests of the loved one; people-pleasing love allows others to continue a behavior that hurts them. Second, true Christian love is given freely; people-pleasing love is given compulsively. Finally, true Christian love is always unconditional; people-pleasing love has strings attached, because the giver wants love and acceptance in return.

To be sure, these insights can be used selfishly. I recently listened to a man on the radio explaining why he never gave money to the poor. "I don't want to become codependent on them by maintaining their habit of begging," he said. That's nonsense. Generosity to the poor does not usually help the poor maintain bad habits; it provides them with essentials. Of course it is wise to give food rather than money to an alcoholic; but to give freely from a generous heart is the mark of love, not codependency. Mother Teresa is not a victim. She gives herself in service to the poor not out of a need to be liked or controlled, but freely, out of love for Jesus. She does not try to manipulate poor people by giving to them, but rather treats them with respect.

Starting to Grow

What is a people-pleasing Christian to do? There are a number of steps in the healing process, several of which have already been described.

The beginning is to make a thorough evaluation of oneself. The outer victim role that forms the character must be seen clearly. The loss of the assertive, decision-making parts of the self into a suppressed assertive role must be acknowledged.

Second, persons who have been trained to disdain the inner voice of the suppressed self as "the flesh" must change their thinking. To break free, the person must stop denying this inner voice and recognize that the suppressed role has the potential for good once it submits to the reign of Jesus. The assertive role has a place in the Christian's life.

Third, the suppressed role's appropriate anger at past injustices must be acknowledged and validated. (More specific guidelines on how to resolve anger follow in the next chapter.) Only then can the suppressed role let go of anger and forgive, paving the way for it to be safely invited "out."

At this point the victim role must face his need for the forceful characteristics of the suppressed assertive self. He needs to see that people-pleasing is bad for himself and for others. When this happens, the two parts of the self learn to appreciate one another. The victim learns to say, "Without you I will never be able to say no or to have an honest relationship. Without you I can't make decisions. Without you I cannot be a real person. I need you." The assertive role, in turn, learns to respond, "I need you too. I appreciate your gentleness and willingness to serve. You are patient when I get irritated. Let's work together."

Next comes the actual emergence of the assertive role in a situation where a strong hand is needed—often a confrontation with a spouse or someone else who the victim feels is taking advantage of her. Anita's experience helps illustrate the kind of process I am talking about.

Holy Confrontation

Anita's white BMW, perfect makeup and sophisticated dress gave her a confident air. When she came to me for counseling, however, that façade soon collapsed as she poured out her frustration with her husband. He was a wonderful material provider; she and her two small children lived in luxury. The one thing he wasn't giving her was himself. Seven days a week he left for work before his family woke up; seven days a week he returned, exhausted, late at night. Even after he had a mild heart attack, he refused to miss much work time. He hid his heart condition from his business associates because he was in line for a top position and ill health might spoil the opportunity.

As I talked with Anita, a familiar pattern unfolded. Her father was a "workaholic" businessman who died in his late forties from heart failure. She saw the situation being re-created in her marriage and was frightened that history would repeat itself.

Anita, of course, was deeply codependent. She had developed expensive tastes during her own childhood, paid for with money earned by her own absent, always working father. When she married, she found a husband who also worked constantly and showed his love for her by buying her things. She appreciated the lifestyle he provided, unaware that she was feeding her husband's addiction to achievement in the workplace, which helped keep down his feelings of worthlessness.

When the children came, it added to his load. In his mind, love meant working even harder to provide things. He had reached the point where his family barely knew him. Now at last the expensive things were unsatisfying for Anita; she wanted her husband more.

With my help, she began to encourage her assertive role to emerge. Eventually we planned a major confrontation between them. Anita found it excruciating even to think of crossing her husband, but she was desperate. For the first time in their marriage she resisted his addictive behavior: "I can no longer go on this way. I am willing to accept a lower standard of living. I cannot watch you killing yourself any longer. I ask you to cut back to no more than a fifty-hour, five-day work week."

It didn't fly. Her husband was highly competitive, and he wanted the promotion. He saw her confrontation as a betrayal, and he was angry. She almost gave up and returned to her victim role, but fear of the future kept her going. In her assertive role she escalated the confrontation by giving him an ultimatum to make sure that he took her seriously. She gave him a month to change; if he didn't, she would take their children and go live with her mother. He threatened her and stormed at her, but tearfully she insisted. He refused to comply. "Just a few more months and the promotion will be secure," he said. "Then I'll relax."

She knew his words were the false promise of an addict. One month later she went home to her mother. As a Christian she wanted to avoid divorce, so she prayed constantly that it would not happen. She wrote to him weekly assuring him of her love, but stayed adamant about his need to change. Her loving and assertive personality roles were working together beautifully.

Note that Anita's confrontational behavior was not based on self-assertion alone. Because she was a Christian, love for her partner and concern for his well-being were her ultimate objective. Although releasing the assertive personality role is a necessary first step for a codependent, for whom *any* act of will is alien, assertion quickly turns to selfishness unless it learns to act in love.

For three months Anita continued her confrontational but loving approach. Then her husband was passed over for the promotion and his world collapsed. He couldn't face the failure, which, coming on top of the loss of his wife, was devastating. He couldn't sleep, and soon he found he couldn't face work. He took a week of vacation from the twelve he had accumulated.

During the desperate prayers of that lonely week, he rediscovered his faith. It seemed to split some hard shell, and a new, softer person—a good man who cared about his family more than his career—emerged. As often happens in codependent couples, the emergence of a suppressed role in his wife caused a similar reaction in him. He and Anita agreed to start over.

Over the next three months he really changed. Occasionally, of course, the workaholic role still slips out, but now Anita confronts him immediately. Their pattern of relating as a family has permanently changed, and just in time: Anita's husband's doctor thinks the lifestyle switch saved his life.

People-pleasers *can* change patterns, but it takes enormous effort. Anita had to put the whole of her faith on the line, rethink her whole relationship with God. When I see her now she greets me with a word that has come to mean everything for her: "Grace." Like her relationship with her husband, her relationship with God has grown as she has been able to accept his unconditional acceptance of her entire self. This new confidence in who she is before God gave her the strength she needed to release the suppressed self.

Decisions and God's Will

As we have seen, Christian codependents expect God to make all their decisions for them. At the same time, however, they have a hard time discerning God's will. Guidance is a subject filled with confusion for them. That's why, as the assertive role emerges, the person needs to learn how to make decisions all over again. This chapter concludes with some biblical insights on how we can expect God to guide us in our decision-making.

Pietistic movements have taught that *every* decision must follow God's expressed will. They have emphasized a mystical communion in which the soul becomes highly sensitive to God's slightest intent. The believer who doesn't listen carefully enough is continually in danger of following God's second-best plan. This kind of thinking is a perfect trap for codependents, since it promises them freedom from decision-making and treats the abdication of that responsibility as a virtue. The problem is that it doesn't work that way. They are never sure they are listening to God hard enough, and eventually they get weighed down by a sense of being destined to endure God's "second-best" forever.

In reaction to such problems, the opposite approach has recently been advocated.[1] In this scenario people consult God's will by studying the Bible but don't expect God to speak to them otherwise. They believe all we are entitled to is *moral* guidance from a God who spoke a long time ago in his Word but has now become silent.

It is refreshing to see how sensible the early Christians were in contrast to all this. Consider what happens in Acts 15 and 16. Paul suggests to Barnabas that they should visit the churches in Cyprus and Asia that they had planted—not because he received a special revelation to do so but because he was concerned for their well-being. Then the two quarrel over whether John Mark should be allowed to go with them. They can't agree, so they split up, forming two missions groups.

Did they blow it? No. Evidently God was guiding them in spite of their quarrel.

Paul followed their previous route into Asia, following the Roman road westward through Pisdian Antioch toward Ephesus. He probably intended to board a boat to return home, perhaps one of the Roman galleys that regularly passed that way to obtain grain from Egypt. Each day he traveled west, preaching as he went. Again, as far as we know, no special guidance was given; he just followed the Roman road. Then his group came to the boundary of the province of Asia, and the picture changes: "Paul and his companions traveled throughout the region of Phrygia and Galatia, having been kept by the Holy Spirit from preaching the word in the province of Asia" (Acts 16:6).

When God's special guidance did come, it was not in an esoteric whisper. It was clear and compelling. They were simply not permitted to go on. Paul and company then turned north—again a decision based on common sense rather than a special revelation. After some time they were once again turned away from their road: "When they came to the border of Mysia, they tried to enter Bithynia, but the Spirit of Jesus would not allow them to. So they passed by Mysia and went down to Troas" (Acts 16:7-8). This time they turned west once again, following another Roman road that gave out on the coast of the Aegean Sea. They were far to the north of the trade routes around the Mediterranean coast, and there was no obvious way to go. Then at last Paul received a vision, a call to cross the sea and enter Greece: "During the night Paul had a vision of a man of Macedonia standing and begging him, 'Come over to Macedonia and help us' " (Acts 16:9).

In this way Paul brought the gospel to Europe, one of the most important missionary moves in the Bible. As we have seen, the decision-making process that led to God's will being done in this way often required following human wisdom (based on kingdom principles), with divine intervention being given at a few key points.

Why does God leave room like this for us to make decisions? Wouldn't it be easier to make all the decisions himself and just tell us what to do?

The answer lies in Jesus' profound teaching that God is our Father. We are children being trained to make wise decisions in accord with the Father's plan. These decisions are to be free, not directed at every point as if we were slaves. As we make choices in the light of his goals for our lives and for the world, we are, by grace, conformed to his image.

Our Father is big enough and wise enough to weave honest mistakes into the pattern of "his best." There is no second-best in his plan. "*All* things work together for good for those who love God" (Romans 8:28 NRSV).

At key points we find ourselves against a wall or, like Paul, facing an empty beach. Then we ask God to guide us explicitly and expect him to answer. He does. This procedure is just what a good father does to train his children to be responsible decision-makers. Rather than encourage clinging helplessness, God as a good Father stimulates a robust faith that involves making decisions. Codependents are gently but firmly encouraged by their loving Father to *choose* his will. The emergence of an assertive personality role makes this possible.

The ability to make choices is a great gift. Take responsibility for your decisions and learn to grow as a trusted child of the great King.

12

CULTIVATING A FORGIVING SPIRIT

• • • • • • •

In 1865 *a remarkable meeting took place between the* three most powerful men in the United States: President Abraham Lincoln, General Ulysses S. Grant and General William Sherman. They were looking ahead to the imminent defeat of Robert E. Lee and the Confederate army. I say the meeting was remarkable because of the astonishing forgiveness they showed toward their Southern foes.

They were incredibly different, these three—Sherman quick, nervous and volatile, Grant stolid and unemotional and relentless, Lincoln ranging far beyond them with brooding insights, his profound melancholy touched with mystic inexplicable flashes of light—but each held the faith that the whole country, North and South together, must ultimately find in reunion and freedom the values that would justify four terrible years of war. . . .

When the Southern armies surrendered the two generals would be the ones to say what the terms of surrender would be, and they would take their cue from Lincoln. If the terms expressed simple human decency and friendship, it might be that a peace of reconciliation could get just enough of a lead so that the haters could never quite catch up with it. On all of this Lincoln, Grant and Sherman were agreed.[1]

Lincoln had long sought to promote this forgiving spirit by insisting that the people of the South could have peace as soon as their arms were laid down and the soldiers returned home. General Grant caught the same generous spirit. It led him to pen one of the most magnanimous sentences of American history: "Having gone home, officers and men can stay there not to be disturbed by the United States Authorities as long as they observe their paroles and the laws in force where they reside."[2]

That was written at Appomattox on Palm Sunday 1865 and signed by both Robert E. Lee and Ulysses Grant. At that moment the Civil War was officially over.

After Lincoln's assassination, when vengeful politicians tried to force a federal indictment for high treason on Jefferson Davis and Robert E. Lee, President Andrew Johnson asked Grant, "When can these two be tried?"

"Never," Grant replied. "I have made certain terms with General Lee, the best and the only terms. I will resign command of the army rather than execute any order to arrest him." Nothing more was heard of the indictment.[3]

One of the great regrets of American history is the untimely loss of Lincoln. He alone had the power to encourage that kind of spirit of forgiveness in the Union and perhaps prevent vengeance from being taken on the South, as it was by many people after his death. Some of the scars from those acts of vengeance linger even today.

An ugly, unforgiving spirit poisons individuals as well as nations and states. The damage spreads in widening ripples from the offended unforgiving person to the person who was at fault and out to get those around them. Jesus was absolutely ruthless in denouncing unforgiveness. Let us be quite clear that an unforgiving attitude is wrong.

A bitter, angry personality role can exist inside an otherwise deeply committed Christian, like an island of hate. Most of the time it remains hidden until some perceived injustice brings it to the surface. Then the Christian shell shatters as the angry role emerges for a devastating period. After the tempest the person returns, a little uneasily, to his usual Christian equilibrium. But in the cavern of the mind there lurks the angry personality role, guarding a pile of old quarrels and ancient grudges. By refusing to forgive, he steals the Christian's joy. He must be changed by the power of God.

Jesus' Perspective on Forgiveness

Jesus had lots to say on the subject of forgiveness. One day, for instance, when Peter was probably feeling that he was finally beginning to absorb Jesus' teaching, he posed a moral question and then attempted to answer it himself.

"How many times shall I forgive my brother?" he asked, and then added virtuously, "Up to seven times?"

Jesus' answer was shocking: "Not seven times, but seventy-seven times" (Matthew 18:22). Clearly Peter had another lesson to learn. Jesus' answer opened up a whole new view of forgiveness.

Peter's answer sounded generous, but the spirit it betrayed reeked of legalism. His "virtuous" approach to forgiveness still meant keeping count of offenses. One imagines him gritting his teeth at each offense—and counting. When the count reached eight, virtue would be rewarded and the angry role could administer a heavy reprisal, made all the sweeter by a delightful sense of self-righteousness.

To help Peter and the other disciples understand what he was trying to teach them about forgiveness, Jesus told the following story, recorded in Matthew 18:23-35.

A great lord had a servant who amassed a debt of several million dollars to his employer. Eventually the servant grew frightened at the enormity of the amount. Even if he worked for a lifetime or sold himself and his family into slavery, he still could only pay a small part. In desperation, he finally went to his master to talk about it.

To the servant's absolute astonishment, his lord didn't seem to get angry when he explained that he could never pay him back. He waited tensely for the blow to fall; perhaps the master's kind facial expression was meant to be sarcastic.

"Come here," ordered his lord. *This is it,* the man thought. *He'll demand my life.*

"Be patient, Lord," he pleaded, falling to his knees. "I will try and pay you back as much as I can."

"I am going to cancel the debt," his employer said. "It's all right. I forgive you."

The servant could not believe his ears. Hope replaced despair in his heart and blossomed into joy on his face.

The very next day the man met another servant who owed him ten dollars. Crossing the street in three quick strides, he confronted him.

"You have been avoiding me," he said to him. "I insist that you pay me back this instant."

When the fellow servant protested that he could not yet pay him, the man flew into a rage. "You *will* pay me," he said, grabbing his throat. He began to choke the life out of the other man. The crowd restrained him physically, but, still in a fury, he had the fellow thrown into debtors' jail. All over ten dollars!

When the lord heard about this, he grew very angry. "I forgave your million-dollar debt, and you could not forgive your fellow servant a ten-dollar debt?" he cried. "Now you too will be put in debtors' jail and remain there until every penny of your own debt is cleared."

Turning People into Stones

I wonder how Peter took this story. His ideas on forgiveness all seemed so reasonable before Jesus' story. Now he didn't feel virtuous at all—just cheap. Suddenly his "generous" sevenfold forgiveness looked shoddy.

I can identify with Peter and even with the wicked servant in the story. What about you? Most of us just can't escape from our habits of counting credits and insisting on our rights; they seem so reasonable. In Jesus' story the unforgiving servant looks really mean, of course, but when you or I are in the grip of an angry role that wants reparation, everything looks very different.

Don't you ever find yourself feeling a sneaking sympathy for the wrong side in Scripture? Take the Pharisees. After all, they had tried very hard to build a life of righteousness, and it was difficult work. How dare Jesus suggest that repentant drunkards and prostitutes were equal in God's sight with them! Then there's the elder brother in the parable of the prodigal son. He may not be very attractive, but his argument seems reasonable enough to us when we are in this kind of mood. Why *should* the prodigal be allowed home so easily? Surely throwing a party for him is going way too far. Shouldn't he be made to wait a little and to worry, so that he will learn his lesson? Yet no matter how reasonable such thinking sounds, we feel a little uneasy agreeing with Jesus' enemies. After all, that makes us Pharisees too!

When we have been cheated or mistreated, it is natural for our angry personality role to feel a burning sense of outraged injustice. Like the unforgiving servant, we have been trained by society to think in terms of debts being paid and justice being carried out. Yet Jesus' story condemns his unforgiving attitude.

If you have been badly hurt by others, it isn't easy to forgive them, especially if they "got away with it." If you were left with the children while your spouse skipped town to have a good time with someone half your age, it's hard not to get bitter (especially if the scoundrels end up seeming happy!). If your teenager left after nearly destroying your peaceful home, your family, your career and your peace of mind, it may be hard to get enthusiastic about taking him back when he comes crying to you for help. It's difficult to keep the angry role from berating him and making him "pay" for what he did.

If your girlfriend has left you and you find she's been sleeping with your best friend, if your boss's best friend's son got your promotion when everybody knows he doesn't work half as much or half as well as you do, it's rather difficult to keep from feeding an unforgiving personality role, isn't it?

Jesus' story shows that you can live by law if you want to, keeping tallies of the injustices you have suffered. You can indeed claim your rights. But if you choose that path, be prepared to face your Maker one day as your Judge. Remember then that it was *you* who chose to go to court. Jesus insists that if we seek forgiveness, we must understand what we are asking for. Really understanding his forgiveness means letting go of our own grudges, complaints and bitterness. You cannot be forgiven your own mistakes if you insist on demanding all that is due to you from others.

The Root of Bitterness

As always, listening to Jesus is good for you emotionally as well as spiritually. As the years go by those old grudges never die; they fester in the dark caverns of your mind where the angry personality role lives. He gets more powerful as the ugly pile of grudges grows. Soon the resentment and bitterness seep through the cracks and begin to show on the outside. As time goes by the lines on your face and the whine in your voice will show how much of you has been taken over by your unforgiving spirit.

Forgiveness brings healing. Jesus knows that and loves to dispense it with his own bright and burning joy. Because forgiveness is a powerful thing to let loose in one's life, however, we often find ourselves objecting to it. "But Lord," we say, "it's not reasonable."

Why do the arguments of the unforgiving personality role look so reasonable and Jesus' forgiveness so impractical? It is because he challenges our self-righteousness. Deep down we long to feel it; it springs into life with every real or imagined offense against our rights. Then when nothing happens to the offender as punishment, we become bitter—still believers, but bitter.

This tendency to become bitter over mistreatment often takes root in childhood. That's why the wise old Word warns parents not to embitter their children (see Colossians 3:21). Because parents hold power over their children, little ones are very vulnerable to feeling anger over being unfairly treated—all the more so because they have very little recourse but to take the abuse. Did you experience those feelings as a child?

Every child knows that she is entitled to loving, caring parents, and when parents fail (or even seem to fail), the child feels cheated. Did your parents take the love that should have been yours and give it to your sister or brother? Were they too busy pursuing their careers to pay attention to you? You tried and tried but never seemed to receive the love you needed, and you were filled with a burning sense of injustice.

The root of bitterness begins with this righteous anger we feel as children when this happens to us. This sense of injustice, combined with our powerlessness as children, engenders deep anger. Because children's expressions of anger are so often punished, their angry inner selves usually go underground. On the surface all may appear well; the child is submissive to parental authority, and the parents are proud of that fact. But beneath the surface a weed of bitterness has taken root.

Often this bitter weed bursts into full bloom during marriage. That's why the Bible commands, "Husbands, love your wives and do not be harsh with them" (Colossians 3:19). Wives have expectations of their husbands, and we husbands often fall short of them. If our wives feel that we are taking out our inner anger on them by being harsh, however, a seed of bitterness is planted.

The wife who experienced bitterness when she was rejected as a child now finds her husband behaving as her father once did. The angry personality role gains strength and expresses itself in uncooperative, unforgiving ways.

It works the other way too. The world is full of men whose wives have assumed control over them, acting like mothers— angry, controlling mothers—instead of wives. Such a man who was initially resentful of his mother transfers his resentment to his wife. The angry personality role generated in his childhood now begins to undermine his spouse as once he undermined his mother. On the surface he may seem to cooperate with her, as the passive personality role plays its part. But sooner or later his resentment over being emasculated grows, and along with it his bitterness. That's why the Bible instructs married women to "submit to your husbands, as is fitting in the Lord" (Colossians 3:18).

It is easy to get defensive about being unforgiving. Others *have* done terrible things to us. We feel as if we have a right to be bitter. It's important to remember, however, that there's a big difference between getting angry and being bitter and unforgiving. Nothing is wrong with anger when it is expressed appropriately; it is, in fact, a God-given emotion that can help us grow toward wholeness when it's handled correctly. But holding on to anger in a bitter, unforgiving way hinders our spiritual and emotional growth. Often such bitterness, left to grow, builds a wall of emotional distance around our hearts to prevent us from getting hurt again.

But what is the right way to handle anger at others? Anyone ready for heart-softening surgery?

Giving Anger to God

Jesus told his parable to get Peter and us to shift our perspective on the issue of forgiveness. Peter's angry personality role needed to see his relationships with those who had sinned against him in the light of Jesus' forgiveness of himself.

As I have established throughout this book, then, the way to handle an angry role properly is not to try to kill it (which is impossible) but to retrain it. The personality role, after all, isn't inherently evil; it is angry about injustice, and such anger can be appropriate. The angry personality role becomes a problem only when it is not allowed to express itself and the original injustice is left unaddressed.

Express your anger in the presence of a supportive Christian friend or counselor, and then pray for the strength to let it go. Ask God to make you a forgiver. Lift up your eyes from the molehill of the offenses against you to the mountain of your offenses against God. And then remember that he took the mountain away.

God created us for himself, to delight in us and to enjoy a love relationship with us. We have all responded by rejecting him and trying to usurp his authority. Our selfishness begins showing itself before we even leave home for school. At school and in the marketplace, our pridefulness is encouraged. In our mean and selfish acts we all crucify Christ. The debt that we owe our God grows and grows, like the servant's debt in Jesus' story.

Are those mere words for you? Or have you begun to see the glory you were meant to be for him, so that human sin, your sin, has become vile to you? Have you grasped how much we have cheated God by what we have done? Then match that over-whelming debt with his amazing generosity. His response to our offense was love, and in his love he gave himself in Jesus. After all that we did to him, he chose to love us still—not to withdraw as we tend to do, but to become even more vulnerable.

So he gave himself into our power and we killed him, as he knew we would. In that act of human rejection he declared his love in blood. Countless men and women with hearts of stone have come face-to-face with that love, and as they saw what it means, the blood softened the stone.

A Terrible Love

God died for love of you.

Once you really grasp the glory of that, your life is changed forever. No mountain is too high to climb for him, no task too great. That is how you feel once you have penetrated in despair to the dark center of your being and found that he was there with you, filling your darkness with his light.

Down through the centuries, men and women by the millions have lived and died for love of Christ. Have you ever wondered at this amazing flow of loving sacrifice poured out for him? Wonder no more. You are hearing the song of souls set free.

Don't think his love has finished its work after covering your mountainous debt, for that is only the beginning. His loving commitment to our growth as people is ongoing. In this love he earnestly calls us to the very best, for nothing but the best is good enough for us, his beloved. He begins his work within us to change us, to make us more beautiful in spirit, to build kindness and generosity in us. He works to make us into what he planned us to be from the start.

This love can be a terrible thing. It is no small matter to have our God walking by our side, insisting uncompromisingly on our good. When we settle for mere decency—trying to suppress our anger rather than dealing with it honestly, for example—he urges us on to all-out goodness.

Life is a lifelong surgery in the hands of this Master Surgeon. All of our experiences, especially the painful ones, become part of the daily cutting and shaping that makes us more Christlike people. This is why the Jesus of the Gospels sometimes seems so ruthless—real love is like that. In his eye, you are not only broken, but much too valuable to leave that way. Undergoing this mending process is part of what it means to be God's friends. And that is one reason he has so few.

No one who has experienced the love that exists among Christians who are letting God do this difficult work in their lives ever forgets it. Unbelievers have been remarking on it since the beginning of the church. In the Roman Empire, a society in which life was cheap, those early Christians were different. They visited prisoners, saw that the poor were helped and even buried those who could not afford a funeral. In an age where unwanted babies were left out to die, they did not share in the slaughter. Pagans saw it and were impressed. Tertullian, a historian of the early Christian era, noted that believers made a lasting impression: "Behold how these Christians love one another," people remarked.

Recognizing Your Choice

The choice facing my angry personality role is now clear. If I choose to accept the removal of my enormous debt to God, I must also choose to be a forgiver. It is not two decisions I face, but one. Being forgiven *means* desiring to change to be like him; it *means* living as a forgiver; it *means* lying down on his operating table. There is no other way to be forgiven.

My angry personality role must be drawn into God's circle of love and forgiveness. Recall Jesus' words: "Forgive us our debts, as we also have forgiven our debtors. . . . For if you forgive men when they sin against you, your heavenly Father will also forgive you. But if you do not forgive men their sins, your Father will not forgive your sins" (Matthew 6:12, 14-15).

On one level, simple consistency *demands* that we Christians forgive others—an idea that appeals to personality roles committed to the idea of justice! It was lack of consistency in the unforgiving servant's behavior that made him look so despicable.

On another, more important level, Jesus wants us to become forgivers *because he wants us to become like him.* When we come to him for forgiveness and find him so generous to us, he confidently expects us to throw away our old mean attitudes and choose to be like him. To choose otherwise is to try to exploit God, as if his forgiveness were weakness. That he will not permit.

John put it this way: "Since God so loved us, we also ought to love one another" (1 John 4:11).

But how, realistically, can we become like Jesus? I know from experience that I can't just will it to be so. Where will I get the strength to forgive those who have hurt me? How can I pull out the root of bitterness from my angry personality role?

The answer is simple: I can't. You can't either. But the Holy Spirit can. When you came to him for forgiveness, God implanted a new source of power within you that is still there. He implanted himself. The power to love *is* yours now, for what God requires from you he also provides. "God has poured out his love into our hearts by the Holy Spirit" (Romans 5:5). You are not alone in your efforts to love and forgive.

As we know, Corrie ten Boom spent time in the Ravensbruck concentration camp during World War II. Afterward she told her story in many meetings. After she spoke at a gathering in Berlin one evening, a tall German man came up to her. Hesitantly, head down, he began: "I was one of the guards of Ravensbruck. I was there at the time you were a prisoner. Last Christmas I accepted Jesus Christ as my Savior. I repented of my sins but then I prayed that God would give me the opportunity to ask one of my victims for forgiveness! That is why I am here. Will you forgive me?"

This was a testing time for ten Boom. She had taught the people being rehabilitated at her house of healing in Bloemendaal that true healing could come only when they forgave their enemies. But as she stood face-to-face with her former enemy, she found that deep in her heart an angry personality role had not forgiven all that had happened in the past.

Corrie looked into the face of this man standing there in a dark gray overcoat—the very color reminded her of Ravensbruck. As she remembered from the past his uniform and the peaked hat with the skull and crossbones insignia, a coldness came into her heart. Memories of her sister Betsie and the degradation of their sufferings flooded into her mind. She remembered

Betsie's death in the camp.

There was no forgiveness in her for this man.

Then she prayed: "Jesus help me! I can lift my hand. I can do that much. You supply the feeling."

With difficulty, Corrie put her hand into her former guard's hand and instantly a miraculous thing happened. A warmth shot down her arm into her hand, the warmth of the healing power of the Holy Spirit. It brought tears to her eyes and she said:

"I forgive you with all of my heart!"⁴

Making Lovers out of Believers

So far I have stressed what God has done and can do in you. What about your role in all this?

Your angry personality role will be changed as you consciously choose to forgive. It won't be easy. It will require determined effort from you. Practically it means that you must consciously model yourself on Jesus. The point of your daily Bible study is not to make you knowledgeable about Jesus, but to make you like him. That will only happen as you study the way Jesus behaved and try to copy it in practice. Is that how you read the Gospels?

As you read, ask yourself: "Why did he say that? Why did he do that?" Don't let go of your questions until you find an answer. Then, when you do, come to him and say, "That's what I want to be like today and for the rest of my life. Please help me."

Men and women who do that, day after day through life, begin to reflect Jesus and his love. The face that smiled as he straightened the back of a crippled woman, forgave an adulterous woman and soothed a worried father is seen in them.

As you enter this process, life will become much more exciting. You will find yourself in the exhilarating position of being a worker alongside the Holy Spirit. You will begin to speak his love and forgiveness just when they are needed. Can you think of yourself that way? Can you think of your family members being this way?

Has God given you an angry mother? Then he must want you to act out his forgiveness by forgiving her. Has your husband behaved badly? Then God wants you to express his love by forgiving him. Has your teenager gone wild? Then God wants you to express his love as you firmly but lovingly insist on the best for him and offer forgiveness. Have you been wronged by members of your church? Then God wants you to teach them a new lesson by your actions. You can begin a ripple of forgiveness that will spread.

Will you do it?

Put this book down and take up a telephone or pen. Say "I forgive you" to a parent, spouse, child or friend—whoever you feel a grudge against. Let the healing water of Jesus' forgiveness sweep out all those old, cold grievances. Let his love shine out.

When Forgiveness Is Rejected

Sometimes people don't want to be forgiven. This often occurs when we confront family members whom we remember as abusive. Insisting that they were not abusive at all, they may angrily reject us. This is tremendously frustrating. It was so difficult to face them, and now we feel more abused than ever. Our angry personality role says, "I told you so."

If this happens to you, don't give up. You are not responsible for your abuser's decision, only for your willingness to forgive. Remember what lies inside and outside your self-boundary, which was discussed in the last chapter. Even God's forgiveness doesn't work for those who reject their need of it.

Sadly, rejected forgiveness prevents you from healing the relationship. You may have to live estranged from your former enemy, keeping your distance and holding out the offer of reconciliation. You can do no more under these circumstances. Love calls you to pray for your abuser and to live in hope; it does not require you to pretend that all is well. Injustice can then be faced, recognized and let go. You are free from a burden, even in this unaccepted forgiveness, for the one who has hurt you no longer controls you.

I'm reminded of Alice, who wrote a letter to her father forgiving him for years of sexual abuse. She sent it to him after he had been imprisoned for his incestuous crimes. Because he had never admitted the evil that he had done before going into prison, Alice's heart rose in hopeful expectation when she got a letter from him in return. Wanting to be free of bitterness had prompted her to write her letter in the first place; she hoped that reading the letter from her father would enable her to find reconciliation and resolution as well.

To put it mildly, the letter did not help bring reconciliation and resolution. It was a tirade of hate and manipulation. There was no word of acknowledgment of her forgiveness.

Alice's father would not let her forgive him, because that would have meant admitting his guilt. She will have to stay away from him until he changes—and that may be for life.

Was forgiving him worth it? Alice thinks it was. Because she released her anger, she is free of his control. He can no longer pull her strings in the same way he did, for though she is sad, she is no longer bitter. Even one-sided forgiveness is a blessing.

Appendix 1
INTERPRETING
ROMANS 7

• • • • • • •

In choosing *to discuss Paul's psychology in the* context of Romans 7, I am very conscious of working with a passage whose interpretation is heavily debated. In this appendix I will examine this debate in an attempt to justify views expressed about Romans 7 in chapter four of this book.

Until recently it was believed that in writing his letter to the Romans, Paul was opposing a Jewish belief that salvation was a reward for keeping the law. This was defined as "salvation by works." Since E. P. Sanders's landmark work *Paul and Palestinian Judaism*[1] it has been impossible to maintain this view. Sanders showed definitively that the Jews never believed that they were brought into the covenant by keeping the law. Rather, law-keeping was a privilege of the nation that had *already* been chosen by God's free grace. As they reminded each other at the yearly Passover, Israel was not chosen for its goodness but solely by

God's merciful, undeserved favor. Keeping the law was the way a person responded to the fact that he or she was already in the covenant—not a method of gaining entry into it.

I have followed this widely accepted understanding. In light of it, my layout of Romans as a whole (pp. 52-54) is not controversial. (See, for example, Ernst Käsemann's similar analysis in his *Commentary on Romans.*[2]) Romans 7, then, can be divided into three sections: the introduction (vv. 1-6); the question, Is the law sin? (vv. 7-13); and the inner struggle (vv. 14-25). Let's look at each of these sections in turn.

The Introduction: Romans 7:1-6

Do you not know, brothers—for I am speaking to men who know the law—that the law has authority over a man only as long as he lives? For example, by law a married woman is bound to her husband as long as he is alive, but if her husband dies, she is released from the law of marriage. So then, if she marries another man while her husband is still alive, she is called an adulteress. But if her husband dies, she is released from that law and is not an adulteress, even though she marries another man.

So, my brothers, you also died to the law through the body of Christ, that you might belong to another, to him who was raised from the dead, in order that we might bear fruit to God. For when we were controlled by the sinful nature, the sinful passions aroused by the law were at work in our bodies, so that we bore fruit for death. But now, by dying to what once bound us, we have been released from the law so that we serve in the new way of the Spirit, and not in the old way of the written code.

Paul begins by establishing his basic premise: Christians are no longer under the authority of the law of Moses. They have died to the realm where law (and sin and death—see Romans 6:2-4) reigns: "So, my brothers, you also died to the law" (7:4). This was an offensive statement to a law-keeping Jew, who prized obedience to the law as a privilege. Keeping the law is what marked him off as one of God's covenant people, Israel. How could it be classed with sin and death as an oppressive alien power?

This question, Is the law sin? is addressed in the remainder of Romans 7. In the forefront of Paul's mind is the role of the law. He himself had earnestly striven to keep it as a response to the grace that had caused him to be born into the covenant of Israel. Paul had concluded from his own experience that this approach to the law led only to frustration and compulsive behavior, which he describes in poignant terms later in the chapter.

When we speak about where Paul is and isn't referring to his own personal experience in Romans 7, we immediately enter the ground that has been so hotly debated. The first-person language of this chapter is filled with intense anguish, yet the Paul who wrote the indisputably biographical third chapter of Philippians shows no such anguish. This has caused many scholars to reject the idea that Paul is here showing how before his conversion he wrestled with internal tension (the so-called psychological interpretation). In its place a "communal" interpretation has become popular. In this view, Paul's "I" represents humankind under the Fall. To be sure, undertones in the passage do suggest that Paul is speaking about the Fall.

I believe that he *is* writing about archetypal human experience; but that does not mean he couldn't have been speaking from personal experience as well. Indeed, it is highly likely that he is speaking about both archetypal human experience and his own personal experience here. One can write convincingly about one's own experience without appealing to the archetypal human experience; but one cannot write convincingly about the archetypal human experience without appealing to one's own experience. In addition, to say that Paul was speaking only of human experience in general certainly does not explain the passion of this passage.

Once the personality-role pattern is understood and combined with the rabbi's *yetzer* theology, the difference between Philippians 3 and Romans 7 is explicable. It is no longer necessary to run away from the plain meaning of the "I" language in both chapters.

Thinking about Paul's introduction this way also helps us see how it helps prepare the ground for Romans 8, where Paul describes the new realm of freedom from the law. In this chapter we are suddenly in a different world. The frustration is now absent, although the struggle with the flesh goes on. In Romans 7 I am "unspiritual, sold as a slave to sin . . . a prisoner of the law of sin" (vv. 14, 23) and unable to carry through on my desire to keep the law. In Romans 8 I have been "set free from the law of sin and death"; in the new life of the Spirit "the righteous requirements of the law" can be "fully met" (vv. 2, 4). The law is relegated to the old life along with sin and death. There remains a struggle, but it has a different character. There is a hopeful tone about the outcome, for "you . . . are controlled not by the sinful nature" (v. 9). We are no longer under "obligation . . . to live according to . . . the sinful nature," for if we do, we "will die" (vv. 12-13).

Still, Paul is conscious that the law is God's law and is therefore "holy, righteous and good" (7:12). How, then, could God's law have ended up being associated with the old regime of frustration and death? That is the question Paul is answering in the remainder of chapter 7 through his anguished description of life under the law. He genuinely cares about his fellow Jews caught in the same trap that once held him (compare Romans 9:2-3). For this reason Paul uses first-person or "I" language throughout the balance of the chapter.

Paul ends the introduction by coming back to the analogy that begins it: our relation to the law is compared with the marriage bond. In verses 5 and 6 Paul looks back on his days before becoming a Christian (when he was controlled by the sinful nature) and shows how the law worked to tempt our bodily appetites to sin. In verse 6 he speaks as a Christian ("we have been released from the law") who can serve God "in the new way of the Spirit." In other words, Christians, like a wife whose husband dies, are no longer married to the law, for it has died for them. Note the "we" language that Paul regularly uses[3] to address fellow Jews "who know the law."

Is the Law Sin? Romans 7:7-13

Having established his basic proposition that Christians are freed from the law by dying to it in Christ, Paul now moves on to his question about the law:

> What shall we say, then? Is the law sin? Certainly not! Indeed I would not have known what sin was except through the law. For I would not have known what coveting really was if the law had not said, "Do not covet." But sin, seizing the opportunity afforded by the commandment, produced in me every kind of covetous desire. For apart from law, sin is dead. Once I was alive apart from law; but when the commandment came, sin sprang to life and I died. I found that the very commandment that was intended to bring life actually brought death. For sin, seizing the opportunity afforded by the commandment, deceived me, and through the commandment put me to death. So then, the law is holy, and the commandment is holy, righteous and good.
>
> Did that which is good, then, become death to me? By no means! But in order that sin might be recognized as sin, it produced death in me through what was good, so that through the commandment sin might become utterly sinful.

Because Paul writes in "I" language in the past tense, he seems to be describing his own past experience. He divides his past life into a time when he was unaware of sin ("once I was alive apart from the law"). Then he came under the law ("when the commandment came") and found that the result was disaster ("I died").

175

When was this time in Paul's life when he was not under the law?

It was customary among the Rabbis to discuss the different ages of a man. In *Pirke Aboth* 5. 24, Judah ben Tema (A.D. c. 150) said: "At five years the Scriptures; at ten years the *Mishnah;* at thirteen the commandments; at fifteen the *Talmud* etc." This saying is regarded as an addition to the Aboth but at the age of thirteen it was generally recognized that a boy is made a "son of commandment"—*bar mitzvah,* i.e. he becomes morally responsible and is received into the community.[4]

In the "age of innocence" Paul was a child, under no personal obligation to keep the law. Instead he was under the tutelage of his father. F. F. Bruce comments: "The day came when Paul had to take upon himself the obligation to keep the law. The occasion might be the *bar mitzvah* ceremony [in which a Jewish boy at the age of thirteen assumes a personal responsibility to keep the law.]"[5] The time when a Jewish boy entered adulthood and became a "son of commandment" was a celebrated rite of passage. It marked the moment when the law took control. From Paul's new perspective as a Christian, however, it was a tragedy, for the very law that was intended to bring life actually brought death (v. 10). Paul is honest about his inability to keep the law.

Thus far Paul seems to answer his startling question—is the law sin?—with an affirmative. Now, however, he makes clear exactly what he means by *sin.* The word here means not mere wrongdoing but an active power that seizes the opportunity to bring about condemnation under the law. It is an alien power active inside our minds that exploits divisions between our personality roles.

Behind Paul's language in this description of his own life there is a universal echo of the fall of Adam and Eve from innocence. "The commandment" (singular) sounds like a description of God's word to Adam: "You must not eat from the tree . . . for . . .

you will surely die" (Genesis 2:17). Furthermore, the first couple's sin was covetousness, the very sin Paul mentions (Romans 7:7-8).

Paul's use of "I" language here does not mean he is speaking only about the human race in general terms. Rather, he speaks of himself personally to underline an essential point: even a Pharisee as rigorous as Paul is caught in Adam's sin, in solidarity with the whole sinful human race. Paul's subtle combination of his own experience with themes from Genesis 3 makes this point powerfully.

As he continues, Paul separates the power of "sin" from the voice of the law. He has now answered the opening question. The law is not sin; rather, sin is an independent agent inside the mind that uses the law to bring the mind down and to take it over. God's purpose in giving the law was therefore to expose the reality of sin in the human heart (v. 13).

The Inner Struggle: Romans 7:14-25

The final section contains an important change. The "I" language is maintained, but the tense changes from the past to the present.

I do not understand what I do. For what I want to do I do not do, but what I hate I do. And if I do what I do not want to do, I agree that the law is good. As it is, it is no longer I myself who do it, but it is sin living in me. I know that nothing good lives in me, that is, in my sinful nature. For I have the desire to do what is good, but I cannot carry it out. For what I do is not the good I want to do; no, the evil I do not want to do—this I keep on doing. Now if I do what I do not want to do, it is no longer I who do it, but it is sin living in me that does it.

So I find this law at work: When I want to do good, evil is right there with me. For in my inner being I delight in God's law; but I see another law at work in the members of my body, waging war against the law of my mind and making me a prisoner of the law of sin at work within my members. What a wretched man I am! Who will rescue me from this body of death? Thanks be to God—through Jesus Christ our Lord!

So then, I myself in my mind am a slave to God's law, but in the sinful nature a slave to the law of sin.

The shift in tense gives this passage an unmistakable note of anguish. In chapter four I said, "The pain is too real for us to treat this passage as a generalization of human existence, as some have tried to do." The anguish of the passage suggests that the "I" must be taken at face value; this is Paul's own experience. What we have is *two* selves or personality roles at war with each other. The dominant religious role tries in vain to suppress the rebel role, and the usual compulsive behavior results.

Paul speaks as one caught helplessly between a desire for good and a rebellious will that overcomes that desire. No longer is "sin" the only villain; it is "I" who keep on doing evil. Yet it is not the same I as the one who wills the good, but an inner opponent. Here is personality-role language at it plainest: a divided will is in anguish over its compulsive behavior.

Thus Romans 7 is not about the war between the flesh and the Spirit in the Christian heart, as many commentators have argued. Rather, it reflects pre-Christian experience. It describes a struggle entirely inside the old nature, which contains both a religious will to do good (as defined by the law) and a will to oppose it. This is the war between the *yetzers* so familiar to the rabbis, with one essential difference: the law and the "good" *yetzer* lose.

The commentators' insistence that Romans 7 refers to Christians has always been justified by the awareness that believers exist simultaneously in the old age of the flesh and the new age of the Spirit. Blinded by the Reformed overinsistence on human depravity, they usually missed the logical consequence of their own position, leaping instead to the conclusion that the only struggle Paul describes is the one between flesh and Spirit. Dunn is a good example;

Paul's strategy is thus beginning to become clear: the split in the believer's "I" corresponds to the double function of the law. There is the willing "I" = the "I" already identified with Christ in his death = the "I" no longer under the law of works but obedient to the law of faith, that is, to the law as spiritual. And there is the impotent "I" = the "I" as a man of the flesh = the "I" not yet identified with Christ in his resurrection = the "I" still under the dominion of the law as used by sin to consign me to death.[6]

The "I" that wills is at once linked by Dunn with "the 'I' already identified with Christ." The impotent "I" is identified with "the 'I' as a man of the flesh." Yet Paul's whole point is that the "I" that wills is precisely the one that is *impotent*. Dunn's confusion is understandable; he is close to grasping that the impotent "I" is *not* the new "I" identified with Christ, but rather a "good" impulse, impotent because it lies within the domain of the flesh and is opposed by another part of the self in the same area, with sin exploiting the division.

The point that has been missed is that the "old man" has an internal struggle too, one that is more painful because it is hopeless. There is a warfare *inside* this domain of the flesh, and since this domain continues to exist for the Christian, the old struggle continues as a civil war between the parts of the flesh. This war is fought alongside the greater war waged between flesh and Spirit. Romans 7 applies to the non-Christian part of the believer ("the flesh") just as much as it applies to the nonbeliever.

Dunn believes that "were it not for sin the double split need never have happened: the 'I' who testifies that the law is good and desires to obey it would be able to translate will into action; the law would be a means to life, and death would have not triumphed."[7] This misses Paul's point entirely. The first "I" was part of the problem. The "I" that wanted to obey the law is *not* uniformly good in complete contrast to a thoroughly evil, sabotaging "I." That is exactly the illusion Paul is out to oppose. Paul's concern is that the "good" part that wanted to keep the law had its own characteristic sins—the sins of pride and exclusivity that keeping the law so often encouraged. Thus even the "good" personality role offers no hope for righteousness. This explains why the key to winning the war of Romans 7 is not killing the opposing personality role, as the religious person expects, but rather the fresh start in the Spirit described in Romans 8. Indeed, only in this way can we explain the transition from Romans 7 to Romans 8.

In Romans 8 Paul addresses a higher level of struggle between the old life of the flesh and the new life in the Spirit. As the Spirit rebuilds more and more of the person into the new life, the struggles of the old life are reduced. In this way the reign of Christ extends in the Christian's life as sanctification proceeds. This doesn't happen *inside* the domain of the flesh. Instead that domain shrinks in extent. The old battle between the personality roles or *yetzers* continues as intensely as ever, but in a smaller and smaller territory. Thus we have the contrast between the slavery of 7:14-24 and the assertion of 8:14: "Those who are led by the Spirit of God are sons of God." Only by becoming "the new man" can we reach the calmer waters of Romans 8 and the new battle in which we are free of "obligation . . . to the sinful nature" (8:12).

Other Views of Romans 7

The Reformed view of Romans 7 agrees with my interpretation for the first six verses but differs radically from it from verse 7 onward. As pointed out above, the anguish is so intense and the language so extreme in this section that it is hard to ascribe it to Christian experience. Words and phrases such as "unspiritual" and "sold as a slave to sin" (v. 14), "what I hate I do" (v. 15), "nothing good lives in me" (v. 18), "a prisoner of the law of sin" (v. 23) and "what a wretched man I am" (v. 24) seem to describe lost humanity rather than Christian experience. Yet Reformed tradition has insisted that Paul is speaking of Christians here. As Calvin says, "He . . . sets before us an example in a *regenerate* man."[8]

In his wonderful book *Knowing God* J. I. Packer put it succinctly: "He had told how, before he was a Christian, 'sin, finding opportunity in the commandment, deceived me and by it killed me'; and he had gone on to review the present in which, Christian and Apostle though he now is, 'I can will what is right, but I cannot do it.' "[9]

This view is supported by Paul's use of the present tense, which obviously suggests that he has now turned to address his current experience as a Christian. Packer believes that Paul uses such extreme language because he is taking the deadly struggle between the flesh and the Christian spirit very seriously: "He had to bear the bitter experience of being unable to attain the perfection he sought, because the law that required it—the law in which, as a regenerate man, he delighted—was powerless to induce it."[10]

In this view Paul's poignant "I" language expresses the anguish of the *Christian* soul newly sensitized to the horror of sin, discovering its tie to the old nature. The resistant rebel self is then the flesh, and the war of Romans 7 is the same as the war in Romans 8.

What's at issue here is bigger than tense and phrasing. Packer and Calvin are fighting for a key principle. Reformed tradition has always argued that the "I" who wills obedience to the law must be the Christian soul. The unsaved soul cannot will the good, because it is altogether evil: "Flesh is what men are called, as they are born and as long as they retain their natural character; for as they are corrupt so they neither taste nor desire anything but what is gross and ugly."[11]

Reformed writers are not simply being negative; their point is a vital one. Every attempt by sinful humankind to stand justified before God by its own efforts must be squashed. Only then can we be faced with our utter inability to keep the law. This was Paul's theme in Romans 3. But is it his theme in Romans 7? I think not.

I do not believe that this gloomy view of the non-Christian soul is realistic. It does disservice to the work of God in the person who has not yet come to faith in Christ. God often works in the heart to bring about a will toward good, long before the soul yields fully to Christ. The Reformers called this work in the unbelieving soul "common grace," but that is a pale phrase for such a necessary part of God's activity. We find this strange mixture of surprising goodness and disappointing wickedness everywhere in the world—including in our own hearts. All sorts of people long for goodness, for God is everywhere at work. If a person yields to a good impulse, then you may be sure that God is at work, for all goodness flows from him. Many non-Christians do long to be better, which shows that God is at work in them too. Consider orthodox Jews. Nobody who has observed their devotion to God's law can doubt their very real longing for holiness. Surely God is at work in their lives.

For this reason we cannot follow the Reformed view and exclude not-yet-Christians from the experience of Romans 7. Often such people yearn for good and are frustrated with the evil they do—the emotions that the chapter captures exactly. The experience of sin as compulsive behavior refers to this very dynamic. The inner tension between personality roles is part of the brokenness of our sinful existence. Sin exploits it to frustrate the good impulses that God encourages in the heart of believer and unbeliever alike.

The motive for the Reformers' insistence on the total depravity of the old self was a worthy one. They wanted to put down the notion that people could perform any act of goodness or even have a desire for goodness on their own. In this way they excluded any possibility of people attaining righteousness independent of God. But their objective can be reached by another route that does not require us to look with such dark suspicion at the behavior of non-Christians. We can assert that God is everywhere drawing all people toward goodness, winning the little victories that prepare the ground for his great final victory of conversion. He is, after all, "the true light that gives light to every man" (1 John 1:9). All we must remember is that responding to God in these acts of goodness in no way enables us to eliminate our sins. With or without such acts we are guilty of rebellion against the throne. The fact that God in his mercy draws me to respond toward goodness does not lessen the sinful state of my heart outside of Christ. Rather, it magnifies the greatness of his grace to think that he works in such alienated hearts. If he did not, how could conversion ever occur?

Once we stop trying to make Romans 7 serve the purpose of exposing human depravity, we are free to see its real function. It is Paul's final note on the anguish felt by the sincerely religious part of the self, longing after God but impotent against its own self-righteousness and the rebel role. It heightens the contrast between the old ineffective struggle of the religious flesh under the law and the new world of the Spirit with its possibility of victory over the flesh, which Paul addresses in Romans 8.

Appendix 2
EGO-STATE
THEORY

•   •   •   •   •   •

Multiple-*personality disorder is defined by the author-*itative American Psychiatric Association's *Manual of Mental Disorders* (DSM-III-R) this way:

> The essential feature of this disorder is the existence within the person of two or more distinct personalities or personality states. Personality is here defined as a relatively enduring pattern of perceiving, relating to and thinking about the environment and one's self that is exhibited in a wide range of important social and personal contacts.[1]

The phrase *personality states* already suggests that a transformation is taking place in our view of the personality as a fully integrated whole. A looser concept of personality as a cluster of discrete states is emerging. More and more, mental-health professionals are asking whether the normal personality's awareness of distinct roles and moods is somehow related to the personality split that true multiples experience.

The segmentation of the personality has been a topic of interest in psychology for a long time. It has come to be known as dissociation, and it now has its own scientific journal *(Dissociation)*. Pierre Janet introduced the term in 1907 to describe systems of ideas that were "not in association" with other normal ideas in the personality.[2] Paul Federn later coined the phrase *ego state* to describe personality segments he discovered in his patients.[3] A person's behavior, in his view, was governed by the ego state currently "executive."

Further evidence of personality segmentation comes from hypnosis. E. R. Hilgard at Stanford University has noted the presence of a "hidden observer" in a hypnotized subject.[4] When a temporary state of deafness was induced in the person, some other part of the personality was still able to respond to a voice. This led Hilgard to propose that hypnosis itself is a form of dissociation. Whether one accepts this or not, the hidden-observer phenomenon is evidence for the existence of different states of awareness within the individual.

Starting with their work on hypnosis, J. G. and H. H. Watkins developed what they call "Ego State Therapy."[5] This is very similar to the ideas presented in this book, despite the fact that they as therapists and academics approach the topic very differently in some ways from the way I do as a pastor.

Like me, they believe in a spectrum of dissociation. They call the dissociated parts of the personality "ego states":

> We have gathered increasing evidence that the dividing of the personality lies on a continuum ranging from normal adaptive differentiation at one end to pathological maladaptive dissociation at the other, where the true multiple personality disorder occurs.[6]

Second, they believe that ego states reveal themselves under hypnosis.

Third, they believe that at the therapist's suggestion, a particular ego state can take a memory (such as an experience of pain) into itself so that other ego states are unaware of it. This is their explanation for posthypnotic amnesia. They point out that such memories are not lost and therefore must exist elsewhere in the mind; hence ego-state division must be occurring.

What Watkins and Watkins have found to occur only under hypnosis I have observed in normal, prayer-based pastoral counseling. These experiences indicate the general usefulness of the approach of Watkins and Watkins and support the conclusions set forth in this book.

Notes

Chapter 2: Which I Is Me?

[1]Pierre Janet, *Les medications psychologiques,* 3 vols. (Paris: Felix Allcan, 1919), trans. as *Principles of Psychotherapy,* 2 vols. (New York: Arno, 1976).

[2]J. F. Masterson, *The Search for the Real Self* (New York: Free Press, 1988), p. 30.

[3]Ibid., p. 23.

[4]Miguel de Cervantes, *Don Quixote of the Mancha,* trans. Thomas Shelton, Harvard Classics 14 (New York: Collier, 1962), p. 22.

[5]Jay Martin, *Who Am I This Time?* (New York: Norton, 1988).

[6]Book review, *San Jose Mercury News,* July 19, 1992.

[7]Paul Federn, *Ego Psychology and the Psychoses* (New York: Basic Books, 1952).

[8]For example, see John Bradshaw, *Healing the Shame That Binds You* (Deerfield Beach, Fla.: Health Communications, 1988), p. 133.

[9]Masterson, *Search for the Real Self,* p. 25.

[10]B. A. Van der Kolk and O. van der Hart, "The Intrusive Past: The Flexibility of Memory and the Engraving of Trauma," *American Imago* 48, no. 4 (1991): 425.

[11]A complete spectrum of dissociation would include other kinds of severe dissociation besides multiple-personality disorder—most important, dissociation caused by a sudden trauma. Because this kind of personality fragmentation differs from the more or less conscious dissociation that is the subject of this book, it has not been covered here.

Chapter 4: The Apostle Paul Looks at Personality Roles

[1]Ernst Käsemann, *Commentary on Romans,* trans. Geoffrey W. Bromiley (Grand Rapids, Mich.: Eerdmans, 1980), 1:200.

[2]This section is a summary of W. D. Davies, *Paul and Rabbinic Judaism* (Philadelphia: Fortress, 1980), pp. 20-35.
[3]Ibid., p. 23.
[4]George Foot Moore, *Judaism*, 3 vols. (Cambridge, Mass.: Harvard University Press, 1927-1930), 1:482.
[5]*Talmud Sukka* 52a.
[6]1QS 11:9, quoted by Käsemann, *Commentary on Romans*, 1:201.
[7]James D. G. Dunn, *Romans 1-8,* Word Biblical Commentary 38A (Dallas: Word, 1988), p. 408.
[8]Ibid., p. 406.
[9]Ibid., p. 408.

Chapter 5: Self and the Christian
[1]Donald Guthrie, *New Testament Theology* (Downers Grove, Ill.: InterVarsity Press, 1981), p. 472.
[2]Millard J. Erickson, *Christian Theology* (Grand Rapids, Mich.: Baker Book House, 1983), p. 341.
[3]Gordon R. Lewis and Bruce A. Demarest, *Knowing Ultimate Reality,* vol. 1 of *Integrative Theology* (Grand Rapids, Mich.: Academie/Zondervan, 1987), p. 272.

Chapter 7: Starting the Inner Journey
[1]Even if Jesus is referring to disciples here, the force of the analogy presupposes his anger at child abuse.

Chapter 8: Seeking Help
[1]M. Scott Peck, *People of the Lie* (New York: Simon & Schuster, 1983), p. 183.
[2]This is, of course, quite possible. In a case reported in San Francisco, Presidio military base child-care workers who had clearly sexually abused children (some of them developed venereal disease) had close connections with those involved in devil worship. The suicide of the main accused person prevented further revelation. Our courts' inability to adapt to the special problems of abused children, the appalling implications of the rituals themselves and the skepticism of a rationalistic society go far toward explaining the failure to provide evidence in any given case.

Chapter 10: Blaming, Choosing and Responsibility
[1]Today *codependent* is often loosely applied to any victimization or addiction occurring in a relationship. It was first used to describe the relational dynamic in alcoholic families. The alcoholic often persuades his entire family to cooperate in keeping his addiction secret. His wife, for example, will call in sick for him and lie to cover the real reason he is unable to work: he was drunk last night and has a hangover. By doing this she is codependent—that is, she

makes it possible for him to escape the immediate consequences of his addiction because she needs to be needed by him in this way. Her husband, of course, is very grateful and will do whatever she wants for a while. Though things may change for a short time, however, they both know deep down that the cycle will repeat itself. The relationship revolves around his addiction.

[2]Mary Armstrong, professor of educational psychology at Houston University, has authored many papers on incest.

[3]Heidi Vanderbilt, "Incest," *Lear's,* February 1992, p. 41.

[4]Pia Mellody et al., *Facing Codependence: What It Is, Where It Comes From, How It Sabotages Our Lives* (San Francisco: HarperSanFrancisco, 1989), p. 41.

Chapter 11: Pleasing People, Pleasing God

[1]See, for example, Garry Friesen and J. Robin Maxson, *Decision Making and the Will of God: A Biblical Alternative to the Traditional View* (Portland, Ore.: Multnomah Press, 1980).

Chapter 12: Cultivating a Forgiving Spirit

[1]Bruce Catton, *The Civil War* (New York: Fairfax, 1984), p. 658.

[2]James M. McPherson, *Battle Cry of Freedom* (New York: Ballantine, 1988), p. 849.

[3]Gene Smith, *Lee and Grant* (New York: New American Library/Dutton, 1985), p. 297.

[4]J. W. Brown, *Corrie: The Lives She's Touched* (Old Tappan, N.J.: Revell, 1979), p. 80.

Appendix 1: Interpreting Romans 7

[1]E. P. Sanders, *Paul and Palestinian Judaism: A Comparison of Patterns of Religion* (Philadelphia: Fortress, 1977).

[2]Ernst Käsemann, *Commentary on Romans,* trans. Geoffrey W. Bromiley (Grand Rapids, Mich.: Eerdmans, 1980).

[3]See, for example, the interplay between *we* and *you* in Ephesians 2.

[4]W. D. Davies, *Paul and Rabbinic Judaism* (Philadelphia: Fortress, 1980), p. xxiv.

[5]F. F. Bruce, *The Epistle of Paul to the Romans,* Tyndale New Testament Commentaries 6 (Grand Rapids, Mich.: Eerdmans, 1963), p. 147.

[6]James D. G. Dunn, *Romans 1-8,* Word Biblical Commentary 38A (Dallas: Word, 1988), p. 407.

[7]Ibid.

[8]John Calvin, *Epistle to the Romans,* Calvin's Commentaries 19, trans. John Owen (Grand Rapids, Mich.: Baker Book House, 1979), p. 259.

[9]J. I. Packer, *Knowing God* (Downers Grove, Ill.: InterVarsity Press, 1973), p. 233.

[10]Ibid.

WINNING THE WAR WITHIN

[11]Calvin, *Epistle to the Romans,* p. 260.

Appendix 2: Ego-State Theory
[1]American Psychiatric Association, *Diagnostic and Statistical Manual of Mental Disorders* (Washington, D.C.: American Psychiatric Association, 1987).
[2]Pierre Janet, *The Major Symptoms of Hysteria* (New York: Macmillan, 1907).
[3]Paul Federn, *Ego Psychology and the Psychoses* (New York: Basic Books, 1952).
[4]E. R. Hilgard, *Divided Consciousness: Multiple Controls in Human Thought and Action* (New York: Wiley, 1986).
[5]J. G. Watkins and H. H. Watkins, *Hypnosis and Ego-State Therapy, from Innovations in Clinical Practice,* vol. 10, ed. P. A. Keller and S. R. Heymen (Sarasota, Fla.: Professional Resource Exchange, 1991).
[6]Ibid., p. 67.